D1044786

Shopaholics

Shopaholics

Serious Help For Addicted Spenders

by Janet E. Damon

PRICE STERN SLOAN

NOTICE: The information contained in this book is true and complete to the best of our knowledge. All recommendations are made without any guarantees on the part of the author or Price Stern Sloan. The author and publisher disclaim all liability incurred in connection with the use of this information.

Price Stern Sloan, Inc.
360 North La Cienega Boulevard
Los Angeles, CA 90048
Manufactured in the United States of America
First Printing

Library of Congress Cataloging-in-Publication Data

Damon, Janet.
Shopaholics: serious help for addicted spenders.

Includes index.
1. Compulsive shopping. 2. Compulsive shopping—Case studies. I. Title.
RC569.5.S56D36 1988 616.85'227 88-17951
ISBN 0-89586-749-4

Foreword

Americans spend a larger proportion of their income than the citizens of any other industrial country. The shopping center is described by millions of us as the primary locus of recreation. Before the average American child reaches the age of 21, he or she will have been exposed to more than a third of a million television commercials. Not surprisingly, then, a growing number of us have difficulties controlling our spending habits.

As Janet Damon persuasively demonstrates, compulsive spending can have many of the same qualities, and can create many of the same problems, as any other addictive behavior. When spending becomes the means to relieve powerful feelings of worthlessness or anxiety, it ceases to be a voluntary activity and becomes a sickness.

Ms. Damon's descriptions of the pain and turmoil that compulsive spending can create are vivid and poignant. She elucidates with great clarity and insight the dynamics of this difficulty. Of particular virtue is her ability to combine an appreciation of the childhood roots of the problem with a recognition of the continuing vicious circles that keep it going. As she shows in illuminating detail, compulsive spending does not only *result* from low self-esteem, it also helps *perpetuate* low self-esteem. The individual who attempts to deal with his or her inner turmoil and distress by buying things ends up feeling ashamed, foolish, and guilty, as well as feeling under still more stress due to the realistic problems that debt and soured relationships bring forth. Then, sadly but all too predictably, he or she tries to erase those bad feelings by again going out and buying things; and the whole sad cycle begins once more.

Based on extensive clinical experience in working with compulsive shoppers, Ms. Damon offers a program to break the vicious circle and enable the victim of this painful and self-defeating pattern to find the way to a freer and more fulfilling life. Her approach is at once empathic and practical. It combines a keen understanding of the individual's experience and its deep psychological roots with a recognition that without clear, pragmatic, and systematic guidelines, all the insight in the world will not lead to change.

The number of people for whom this book will be helpful is very large. Far more people have difficulties with spending than is currently acknowledged. Buying has become a way of life (and often a substitute for life) for millions of Americans. I hope this valuable book gets the widest possible circulation.

Paul L. Wachtel
Distinguished Professor of Psychology
City College and the Graduate Center of
the City University of New York

Author of *The Poverty of Affluence: A Psychological Portrait of the American Way of Life*

Acknowledgments

I would like to deeply thank my colleague and dear friend, Anita Weil, for her invaluable assistance in writing this book. I also appreciate the joy, positive energy, creativity, enthusiasm and support she has exhibited throughout this project.

My admiration goes to Drs. Kenneth Meyer and Jerome Gold of the Gestalt Center of Long Island for their insightful training and dedication to their students. They continue to be an inspiration in both my personal and professional life.

Many thanks to my agent, Faith Hornby, and my editor, Judith Wesley Allen, for their support and commitment to this book.

•

Deep appreciation goes to Dr. Eric Lasser and Karen Lasser, MSW, for their valuable insights and suggestions.

•

Thanks also to Dr. Paul Wachtel for our illuminating conversation during the early stages of this book and the continuous encouragement from both him and his wife, Dr. Ellen Wachtel.

•

To all my friends, who've helped me grow with their faith and belief, from the onset of Shopaholics Limited® to the completion of this book.

•

To Emma and Isidor Eckhaus, my parents, who always encouraged me to write.

•

To Alaric.

•

To my husband, Arthur Atlas, whose patience, humor and love enriches my life and my work.

•

And to my clients, whose courage and commitment are the inspiration for this book.

Contents

Shopping fills an emptiness in my soul.—***Lisa M.***

Introduction

"I don't know where my money goes, but I'm almost $30,000 in debt," said Lisa M. during our first conversation. This young working woman admitted that she went shopping almost every day on her lunch break and on most Saturdays. She frittered her money away, spending $20 for a pair of earrings, $10 for a pair of lacy panties or $15 for a couple of lipsticks. Although she rarely purchased big-ticket items, her compulsive spending resulted in enormous debts, bouts of depression and fights with her husband.

"I'm not in debt," Olivia S. said during our initial talk. "My husband earns a good living and I can afford to spend. But I know there's something wrong. I don't like being alone in the house all day, and I don't know what to do with myself besides shop. So I go off to Bloomingdale's or Saks and buy a lot of things I don't need. Then I feel ashamed of myself afterward. I often don't like what I buy. Sometimes I can't even bear to unpack and look at my purchases, so they just sit in a bag in the back of my closet."

Compulsive shopping can result in self-loathing, depression, financial ruin and marital breakups, yet often it is not considered a serious addiction. T-shirts, bumper stickers and jokes promote the idea that overspending is a harmless personality quirk. However, the following facts indicate the extent of this problem and its consequences:

- Adults spend an average of six hours per week shopping, more time than they spend reading, exercising or playing with their children.[1]

- Over two-thirds of adult Americans visit a regional shopping mall at least once a week.[2]

- The average person's debt is nine times greater than it was in 1960.[3]

- The U.S. has about 82 million credit-card holders, and approximately one-quarter of them don't know how much interest they pay.[4]

- The national credit-card debt in 1986 was about $600 billion, and is increasing at an alarming rate of about $5 billion each month, according to Luther R. Gatling, president of Budget & Credit Counseling Services, Inc., in New York City.

- The amount of money lost in loan defaults by overextended debtors nearly doubled between 1985 and 1986.[5]

There are no statistics yet on how many people are compulsive shoppers, but undoubtedly they number in the millions. This addiction cuts across all barriers, affecting men and women of all ages, races and socioeconomic backgrounds. However, because society encourages shopping, many addicted spenders have not acknowledged their problem—some out of ignorance and some out of denial. Even those who admit something is wrong are often confused about how to deal with their habit.

This book will help clear away the confusion by explaining what compulsive shopping is and how it can be treated. The self-help program in this book has been adapted from the Shopaholics Limited® program I developed in New York City in 1985. By using this program, most of my clients have overcome their addiction. The characters you will meet in this book represent composites of clients with whom I have worked.

If you are an addicted spender, you will no longer feel alone when you read about the experiences of the binge shoppers who overcame their addiction through the Shopaholics Limited® program. By way of introduction, these persons will share their stories with you:

- Lisa, who frittered her money away in order to avoid dealing with the haunting trauma of childhood sexual abuse.

- Olivia, the middle-aged wife of an affluent businessman, who roamed the stores to escape loneliness and emptiness at home.

- Anne, who used shopping binges as a way of getting back at her husband whenever conflicts erupted in their troubled marriage.

- David, who tried to buy friendship by always "picking up the tab," but who worked 70 hours a week to support his successful image and extravagant lifestyle.

- Brad, who binged on flashy outfits for the trendy night spots he frequented, desperately trying to forget feelings of inadequacy left over from years as an obese, "uncool" teen.

- Marsha, a middle-aged mother who tried to buy her way into the art world, adopting the sophisticated image of a "patroness of the arts"—and alienating her family in the process.

- Denise, who spent extravagantly on her new baby in an attempt to compensate for her ambivalent, confused feelings about motherhood.

- 24-year-old Marie, who lived with her parents and spent her paychecks on exercise equipment, hoping a perfect body would bring her a perfect man.

- Richard, who was hounded by debt collectors but continued to spend money for expensive camera equipment. He loved the status and feeling of power it gave him.

- Claudia, the lovely mistress of wealthy older men, who borrowed money from her family to buy designer clothes to impress her lovers.

- Jamie, who bought duplicates of so many items for her kitchen that she had no money for mortgage payments.

- Kim, who went through a sudden inheritance of one million dollars in 18 months!

The courage and success of these people can inspire you to embark on your self-help recovery program. By following the practical, step-by-step advice, you too can free yourself from compulsion. To begin the program, all you need is the desire to spend less and gain control of your life. •

When everything seems to cave in on me, all I can think of is getting to the mall.—***Anne***

Chapter 1

Are You a Compulsive Shopper?

We are bombarded daily by a tantalizing array of items for sale. Everyone is exposed to alluring store windows, display cases, billboards, direct mail catalogs, advertising flyers, and newspaper, magazine and television ads that entice us to buy. Advertisers are handsomely rewarded for creating passionate relationships between consumers and goods—for creating trends and promoting new products until they become "necessities." Even the most sophisticated consumers, free of compulsion, can be seduced by the skillful manipulation of words and images by brilliant advertising executives.

Most people develop a resistance to the momentary appeal of excessive buying. Purchases are weighed with a keen sense of budget and need. Yet for too many others, spending is not just a fleeting temptation: it dominates their consciousness and their lives. Shopping is neither practical nor joyful. It is a compulsion that pilots them into bouts of frenetic shopping and reckless spending.

The following quiz will help you determine if you are simply someone who enjoys shopping or truly a compulsive shopper.

Compulsive Shopper Checklist

1. Do you "take off for the stores" when you've experienced a setback or a disappointment, or when you feel angry or scared?

2. Are your spending habits emotionally disturbing to you and have they created chaos in your life?

3. Do your shopping habits create conflicts between you and someone close to you (spouse, lover, parents, children)?

4. Do you buy items with your credit cards that you wouldn't buy if you had to pay cash?

5. When you shop, do you feel a rush of

euphoria mixed with feelings of anxiety?

6. Do you feel you're performing a dangerous, reckless or forbidden act when you shop?

7. When you return home after shopping, do you feel guilty, ashamed, embarrassed or confused?

8. Are many of your purchases seldom or never worn or used?

9. Do you lie to your family or friends about what you buy and how much you spend?

10. Would you feel "lost" without your credit cards?

11. Do you think about money excessively—how much you have, how much you owe, how much you wish you had—and then go out and shop again?

12. Do you spend a lot of time juggling accounts and bills to accommodate your shopping debts?

If an alarm went off and you answered "yes" to more than four of these questions, chances are you're an out-of-control compulsive shopper. But please don't despair! The self-help recovery program outlined in this book can help you learn to control the compulsion to buy. You can learn to enjoy responsible, compulsion-free shopping.

To further clarify what constitutes addictive spending, let's examine ten characteristic problems in the lives of compulsive shoppers: the anxiety-release-depression syndrome; ongoing chaos; sense of being "lost"; looking for love in all the wrong places; sense of powerlessness; perfectionism; feelings of entitlement; anger and hostility; emptiness; and obsession with money.

Anxiety-Release-Depression Syndrome

"I feel like my boss expects me to be perfect. He yells at everyone, but I can't seem to handle it like the others," said Anne T., a married, middle-aged woman with two children.

"I remember the morning of my last shopping binge," Anne said. "He made a big deal about a minor billing mistake. Well, I managed to control my tears until lunch hour, then I practically ran out of the office and headed straight for the mall. I felt so jittery—I wasn't interested in eating. I felt an overwhelming urge to buy something. When I got to the mall, I felt so confused. I didn't know what I really wanted. So I went into the first store I came across, grabbed three dresses off the rack and bought them without even trying them on. Then I went to a jewelry store and bought two pair of earrings.

"Afterward, I felt a weird mixture of relief and guilt. But later that night, all I felt was guilt. I was so depressed about what I had done, it was weeks later before I could bring myself to open the packages. When I finally did, I realized that I didn't like two of the dresses. I'm a little big in the hips and they weren't flattering at all. The third dress was a print shirtwaist almost identical to one I already had. I was so mad at myself for buying them and then waiting until it was too late to return them."

This was not the first time Anne had run out of her office near tears. While it was true that her job as an executive secretary for an import-export firm was demanding, it was also true that she took the criticisms and imperfections of others and internalized them, blaming herself. When her boss criticized her, she didn't attribute it to his bad mood; she blamed it on her incompetence. When she made a mistake, she didn't say to herself, "Nobody's perfect." Instead she berated herself for being imperfect. The distance needed for perspective is sorely lacking in many overly sensitive perfectionists like Anne.

A similar reaction occurred when Anne was harrassed by her teen-age son, Josh. Like many teens, he complained that his mother didn't understand him. Anne couldn't acknowledge that this is a common complaint among teen-agers. She blamed herself for being a terrible mother. Instead of trying to improve communication with him, she took to the stores to find relief.

Addicted spenders often live with a sense of free-floating anxiety stemming from feelings of inadequacy that build up through the daily stress and pressure of life. They find the desired release from those feelings through a trip to the stores. While shopping, they experience a temporary rush of euphoria mixed with a sense of power and mastery that dispels the tension and anxiety. During those moments the addiction is in full force. Their energy changes, and they experience a sense of recklessness with their actions. In truth, their physiology is altered, and they're grabbing at items with a distorted sense of reality. Logic is suspended during the shopping binge.

If they arrive back home with any appropriate purchase at all, they know it's by sheer luck. The thinking disorder does not respond to budget or need. Once the spree is over, they feel shame, remorse, confusion and finally depression. When the depression begins to lift, the anxiety returns and the unhappy cycle begins again.

Ongoing Chaos

Chaos is prevalent in the lives of shopping addicts, both in their internal and external worlds. Their internal chaos manifests itself in several ways. Some of the most obvious are chaotic thoughts and obsessions about money: worrying about debts and bills, fantasizing about having more money, and scheming to get enough to cover the next shopping binge.

"Sometimes I can't concentrate at work because I'm too busy thinking about money. I get all jumbled up in the head," Lisa explained.

Another layer of internal chaos involves the lack of self-esteem caused by irresponsible spending habits. Shoppers feel out-of-control and ashamed but can't stop the addictive behavior. Ironically, poor self-esteem prompts compulsive shoppers to overspend, further corroding their self-esteem.

At the core of their internal chaos is a sense of worthlessness, which prevents them from asserting their needs and getting what they truly want. Often they experience so much inner turmoil that they don't even know what they want, let alone how to go about getting it. This kind of chaos can lead to unsatisfying relationships at home and at work.

It's a destructive cycle. Compulsive shoppers don't know what they want or how to get it. They go shopping to escape from their dissatisfaction and then feel worse about themselves and their lives afterward.

Some of the external confusion in the lives of shopping addicts is highly visible. Their finances are often in disarray. Many dare not balance their checkbooks or look at their credit-card limit. They shun any information that might interfere with their shopping, even if it means greater confusion.

The chaotic state of their closets is frequently symbolic of their lives. Unopened shopping bags containing unused purchases may be stuffed into the back of a closet. Items that seemed necessary during a binge are often inappropriate; some may even be duplications of items the shopper already owns. Many people have collections of housewares, gadgets or equipment stored in tool sheds, garages, cabinets, corners of various rooms or under the bed, cluttering their homes as well as their minds.

Most compulsive spenders aren't sure exactly what lurks in their closets. They avoid organizing them because it would mean confronting the results of their binges. Sometimes addicted shoppers purposely keep their storage spaces in disarray so their spouses don't know the extent of their shopping sprees.

"Even though I keep my house quite neat, my bedroom closet is an absolute mess. My husband teases me, says I must be hiding a skeleton in the back of it," said Lisa. "Unfortunately, his little joke is not too far from the truth. There's a lot of stuff back there I don't want him to see, to know that I bought. The skeletons of my shopping binges, I guess you could say."

With this rampant disorganization of finances, closets and/or storage space, there can be no real sense of internal order and security. The ongoing chaos creates more anxiety and a greater need for release, so the compulsive shopper goes out and buys again.

Sense of Being "Lost"

Olivia appeared on the outside to be an enviable woman. In her mid-fifties, she retained her attractive figure and was always dressed in subtly expensive clothes. She kept her chestnut hair perfectly coiffed. Her husband provided everything that money could buy. However the material comforts of her outward existence did not ease the pain of her inner world.

"I feel like I'm an emotional orphan. Even when I'm with my family, I always seem to feel alone. I just don't feel connected to anyone or anything," said Olivia. "It's scary."

The root of these feelings was her separation from her deepest, innermost part—her essence. She didn't have a sense of being an adult who could bear life alone and adapt well to its experiences. Rather, she felt like a lost child. The only place to run and hide was the stores.

Many compulsive shoppers, even those with a large network of friends and family, desperately crave attention. They feel so lost and out of contact with the world that the attention fed upon them by store owners or salespeople, who know them all too well, becomes inappropriately important.

"I suppose I know these people are only nice to me because I spend so much in their stores. But sometimes when I feel down, it makes me feel better to go into a shop where they ask me how I am and what I need," explained Olivia.

Without a solid core of self-reliance, it is easy to feel overwhelmed and lost in the world. For many addicted spenders, credit cards serve as anchors to keep them from feeling adrift. The credit cards become symbolic of security, confidence and nurturance.

As children, many compulsive shoppers never developed a sense of security or a sense of self. In their adult lives, they experience a nagging need to return to a safe fantasy home that never existed in reality. Many of the items purchased are adult versions of the security blanket that provides a sense of safety for toddlers straying from their mothers' sight. The security blanket is called a transitional object; it provides a sense of the good mother when she is not there.

Many shopping addicts often feel like lost children, yearning for the presence of the perfect mother who will take care of them and make everything all right. Therefore, the items they buy, whether an expensive stereo speaker or a two-dollar belt, become transitional objects. As the blanket once provided some form of solace and security when away from mother, now the objects they purchase are an attempt to regain the security they yearn for, the security that is lacking inside them.

Looking for Love in all the Wrong Places

Many compulsive spenders do not feel worthy of love and anticipate abandonment. They may be unable to accept the sincere love that is offered by their spouses, so they create distance in a variety of ways. Or their fear of intimacy may cause them to choose partners who are incapable of making deep emotional commitments. By choosing the wrong spouses and not asserting their needs, they validate their fear of being unloved. This feeling propels them to the stores.

Anne's spouse Jeff was a "good" husband—faithful and reliable—but he refused to get involved in her inner life. Whenever she talked about her feelings, he cut her off. He tried to fulfill his obligations to his wife, but he did not realize that part of being a good mate meant providing the emotional intimacy she craved. Her shopping binges were a form of revenge.

"Sometimes I get so mad at Jeff," said Anne. "I want to talk about something, but if it doesn't directly involve him or the kids, he shuts me out. It makes me feel better to go shopping, somehow. It's comforting to have something new."

Anne's husband was also rather critical, just as her father and boss were. She surrounded herself with men who perpetuated her feelings of inadequacy. Being criticized made her feel unlovable as well as incompetent, once again reinforcing her lack of self-confidence.

Many shopping addicts, having never received the unconditional love they needed from their parents, have not truly incorporated self-love. It inevitably follows that they will have problems with intimacy, by choosing the wrong mate, not asking for what they need from their relationships, or not accepting love when they receive it. Therefore, they look for love in the wrong places—the stores.

Sense of Powerlessness

Most compulsive spenders feel ineffectual in their lives. Some don't know what they really want or need or what they're capable of achieving. Others are conscious of their capabilities, but may not feel worthy or up to the challenge of meeting their goals. Many are too entangled in denial to accurately assess their strengths or talents. A fragile ego makes them feel helpless in the face of stress and frustration. To offset the perceived powerlessness in their lives, they grab for mastery in the stores.

Olivia married right after her graduation from a prestigious college and never entered the job market. She supported her husband and now-grown children in their career goals, but never established any goals for herself. Olivia never made a conscious decision to be a full-time mother, she just let herself get swept up by the demands of family life. Lacking the self-confidence to expand out of the domestic world, she convinced herself that she never had any options.

"I wanted to work, but I didn't know what field I would fit into, so I let the years go by. Now I feel too old to start anything," she said.

Although it takes courage and determination, many women begin new careers when they are Olivia's age or even older. It was not her age that was holding Olivia back, it was the fact that she had lived with a sense of powerlessness for so long that the thought of setting goals for herself—of even thinking of her "self"—frightened her.

"I've never had to take care of myself. Frank always helps me make important decisions." By saying this, Olivia demeaned her roles as wife and mother, not giving herself credit for taking care of her children and husband. "The thought of going out on my own at this point is more than I can handle. And what could I really do? The only thing I'm an expert on is shopping," she said.

Perfectionism

When children are deprived of love, security and encouragement toward self-realization, they internalize a feeling of not being good enough, of never measuring up. In order to compensate for this feeling, they create an ideal self that they—or any human being—could never live up to. Then they become perfectionists in every area of their lives. They spend vast amounts of energy attempting to be the perfect employee, spouse, parent, friend. This drains vital energy that could be directed toward developing their inner selves and achieving their outer goals.

The greater the disparity between one's ideal, "perfect" self and who one really is, the greater the sense of powerlessness, lack of self-love and dissatisfaction. When these feelings become overwhelming, a person can feel compelled to attain the "perfect" image through purchases, which might be the trendiest clothes, the finest stemware or china, or the latest in electronic gadgets. Yet nothing is ever quite right or perfect. Styles change, trends shift, technology advances, but the self remains the same. Despite all the shopping, the quest for perfectionism remains, driving the person back to the stores time and time again.

David R., a successful entrepreneur in his mid-thirties, worked an average of 70 hours a week. He found it necessary to work so much because it was difficult for him to delegate authority. Being a perfectionist, he felt he had to do everything himself to ensure it was done right. Even on his rare days off, David was always thinking and worrying about his business.

Despite the prosperity of his company, David had no savings, no assets, no financial security whatsoever—not at all what you'd expect of a "successful" entrepreneur. He spent the money as fast as he earned it. He spent it on cars, a Mercedes and a BMW that he traded in every year for the latest models. He spent it on hand-tailored suits from London, designer shirts, silk ties and even silk underwear. Most of all, he spent money on lavish entertainment, throwing extravagant parties and always grabbing the check on social occasions.

David justified his expenditures by maintaining that his image was important to marketing his business. In truth, however, his extravagance was a result of much deeper issues. No matter how successful he appeared, he never felt good enough inside.

Feelings of Entitlement

"I feel like I'm juggling so much between the kids, Jeff, my job," said Anne. "I do so much, I deserve a lot." Because Anne was not getting for herself what she truly deserved—job satisfaction and emotional gratification—she compensated by overspending. Out of her ever-present feelings of emotional deprivation, which stemmed from her childhood, came feelings of entitlement, of deserving more.

Yet on a deeper level she felt she deserved nothing; therefore, she took no steps to improve the quality of her relationships. Instead, she bought more, which created further problems: fights at home, anxiety on the job, financial worries and ultimately lower self-esteem. Anne felt deprived because she could never buy enough to escape from what she truly needed to do for her life and her relationships.

Most addicted shoppers perceive the world as a place of harsh justice, where a system of punishment and rewards prevails. Shopping and buying are rewards for their deprivation; a way of righting the wrongs from the past and, perhaps, the present as well. Yet their feelings of worthlessness are always at war with their sense of entitlement. With every additional shopping spree, the worthlessness is refueled with more guilt, chaos, anxiety, depression and very often, more debt.

Anger and Hostility

"I never started compulsive shopping until I got married," said Anne. Being angry with Jeff often triggered a shopping spree. She knew it aggravated him when she overspent; it was a way of getting back at him for upsetting her. Just as a child might have a temper tantrum, so might a compulsive shopper. Instead of kicking and screaming, the tantrum is a shopping spree.

Full of self-doubt, Anne felt powerless in her unhappy marriage, afraid to stir up things and make vital changes. This feeling of impotence erupted in occasional bouts of fury and the need for revenge. The only way she knew how to seek revenge was to deplete their bank account by overspending. The depletion of their joint savings account mirrored the depletion of love and understanding within their marriage.

Often the anger of compulsive shoppers terrifies them so much they avoid expressing it at all, even to themselves. They are so afraid of their anger/rage, they can only vent it in the "safety" of the stores.

Emptiness

Olivia had a difficult time being alone with herself. Even though she wasn't always conscious of what she was feeling, the anger and sadness that she was carrying made her very uncomfortable when alone.

"When I'm by myself, I feel so empty and scared," she said. "I hate feeling that way, but I just don't know what to do about it. I've tried to explain it to Frank, but he doesn't understand and that makes me feel worse."

She tried to numb her discomfort by watching television excessively and spending hours on the phone with friends. But her favorite diversion was shopping. She tried to purchase more and more, in an attempt to fill the emptiness inside, but she could never buy the inner contentment that she lacked.

Most compulsive shoppers suffer from a void that cannot be filled, from an internal voice that tells them, "I can't get enough, I'll never have enough!" Shopping binges are the equivalent of gorging on junk food; it's not nourishing or satisfying and only makes them feel worse. Like empty calories, the goods purchased fail to replenish or fulfill, so they return again and again to the stores for more empty refills.

Many compulsive shoppers are trying to buy the happy childhood they never had. Others are buying objects imbued with traits they feel lacking inside. Yet the hollowness is never filled. It persists, piloting the addicted spender into greater debt and deeper despair.

Obsession with Money

Lisa, in debt for $30,000, decided to consolidate all of her loans. This meant that for five years, almost half of her take-home salary would be allocated to repaying her consolidation loan, leaving her little money for shopping. She became obsessed with thinking about how she could possibly survive without her "shopping fix." In order to escape from her grim reality, she began spending hours fantasizing about what it would be like to be rich. This affected her job performance as well as her relationship with her husband. He began to complain that she wasn't paying enough attention to him, that she seemed like she "wasn't really there." Indeed, she frequently wasn't; she was often absorbed in her thoughts.

Lisa knew that her husband's salary and the little she had left over would take care of necessities, but necessities would hardly take care of what she felt she needed. Feeling more and more deprived, she began to scheme. "I actually fantasized about stealing money or stealing clothes from stores. I felt so guilty for even thinking those things, but the thoughts wouldn't go away!"

Most people think about money and worry about it occasionally, but addicted shoppers often do it constantly. Their persistent thoughts torment them, and they feel powerless to stop them. Like a broken record that can't be turned off, the cycle of anxious thoughts goes on and on. They think about how much they owe; how they'll manage to pay off their debts; how much they'll need for the next month, the next year or the next five years. They also dream about what they'd buy if they were rich, losing themselves in long reveries and fantasies about being wealthy.

Obsessive thoughts of money eclipse other outlets for self-gratification. Focusing on money narrows their perspective and their world, when what is really needed is expansion. An obsession with money leaves no room for the compulsive spender to reduce stress and take the steps needed in order to lead a more satisfying life. •

I am not a nobody like my father—just check out this $800 suit!—***Richard***

Chapter 2

The Roots of Compulsive Shopping

There are many reasons why people turn to compulsive shopping. However, when shopaholics in support groups begin to discuss their childhood experiences, they find they share many common problems from their early years. As you read through the following case studies, which reflect major prototypes, you may recognize feelings and experiences from your past. This will give you insight about the roots of your spending addiction and help you realize that you're not alone.

Doting Father/Withholding Mother

Jamie grew up in a working-class family in Cleveland. Her father was a hard-working foreman in a factory that manufactured machine parts. Her mother came from a solidly upper-middle class, better-educated family than his. Her parents married soon after high school, and her father started working. However, his wife expected that he would someday go to college and "make something of himself." Then a baby arrived unexpectedly, and another, and he never had a chance to go back to school. In fact, it was so hard to keep up with the cost of raising children that Jamie's mother had to go to work part-time as a school secretary.

Jamie, the youngest of four, was conceived when her mother was 44. Her mother didn't want any more children, but her husband did. Neither of them believed in abortion, so Jamie was born. "Somehow I always knew I had been an 'accident'," said Jamie.

Her mother did her duty with Jamie, but joylessly. "She'd take me to skating lessons, but she would never watch me like the other mothers did. She'd just sit there and read and then take me home, which kind of ruined the fun. When my father came, though, he'd watch and wave and blow kisses at me. Then after the lesson, he'd come out on the ice and skate with me. He'd spin me around and he'd pick me right up if I fell. It was wonderful."

Her father was a simple, down-to-earth man who loved her unabashedly. He laughed when Jamie did something "naughty" and got angry when his wife punished her. He showered Jamie with compliments and kisses. Her mother frowned on this behavior, saying, "You'll spoil her to death."

He also bought her lavish, sometimes inappropriate presents, which made her mother resentful because of their limited income. "I'll never forget when I was ten, I wanted Barbie's Dream House for my birthday. My mother told me it was too expensive and I needed clothes instead, so she bought me some dresses I hated. My father went ahead and bought me the Dream House, but it turned out to be a nightmare. My mother started yelling at my father, pouring out all this bitterness she felt about having to work because he didn't make enough money, and saying he wasted money on me. My birthday was ruined, and I couldn't even enjoy the dollhouse after that. I felt so guilty." As an adult, she would recreate this misery by buying things she didn't need and then feeling guilty.

The conflicting messages her parents gave her were very confusing. Her father made her feel like a pampered princess, while her mother's attitude was that she didn't deserve anything, even a hug. These dichotomous feelings of entitlement and worthlessness followed her into adulthood: when she felt bad, she'd also feel she deserved something and head to the shops. Later came the letdown.

The mother-child bonding in early childhood that is imperative for healthy development was absent from Jamie's formative years. Her mother was not a healthy model of nurturance, so Jamie was not able to internalize and identify with the "good mother." Being deprived of her mother's nurturing led to her particular form of shopping addiction: buying multiples of items for her bedroom and kitchen.

By the time Jamie was a teen-ager, she was the only child left at home. Her mother pressured her to do well in school. "You better get good grades so you can go to college and make something of your life," she'd say, implying that Jamie's father was a failure because he hadn't. Jamie became a perfectionist because of this pressure, a trait that stayed with her. Later, when her idealized self "failed" her, she'd head to the stores.

Jamie's father had an easier time with his daughter's emerging sexuality then her mother did. Her mother would try to stop her from wearing the mini-skirts that were then in style, but her father would shrug and say, "All the gals are wearing those." He'd say she sure looked pretty when she came downstairs to go out on a date, while her mother would say, "He's going to think you're easy if you wear that." Worst of all, her mother would look on disapprovingly when her father hugged and kissed her, begrudging the demonstrations of affection that made her uncomfortable.

This pointed up another confusing aspect of Jamie's youth—the triangular relationship between her mother, father and her. Whenever Jamie's mother observed the closeness between Jamie and her father, she would become unconsciously jealous. She would give subtle hints of dissatisfaction by interrupting their conversations at important points. She tried to sabotage their relationship in many different ways because she interpreted it as threatening.

This made Jamie uncomfortable and confused, putting her into a no-win situation with her parents. If she was close to her father, she alienated her mother and felt guilty. If she wasn't, she felt the loss of a relationship she treasured. She did remain close to her father, but the triangular situation haunted her into adulthood. She had attendant feelings of repressed rage toward her mother and overall confusion.

Her emotional legacy was a sense of entitlement from her father and a sense of deprivation from her mother. With her first paycheck, she became a compulsive shopper.

Jamie graduated from college with a degree in computer science and went to work in a large company. She didn't enjoy her job because her perfectionism caused her to be so self-critical that the normal pressures of her job were overwhelming.

When she was 25, Jamie married a man who was successful and accomplished. This gave her a sense of security. She became pregnant within months and happily quit her job. However, even after two children and six years of marriage, Jamie and Don were not true partners. She expected more than Don could deliver, because he could never give as much as her father. Also, she identified enough with her mother to have become undemonstrative. Jamie had not internalized the warmth of mother love. Therefore, her marriage lacked the intimacy that she desperately needed but couldn't give or receive. Not knowing how to deal with this lack of intimacy, her shopping binges increased.

Her husband was not fully aware of the ramifications of her compulsive shopping until they had children and she stopped working. As time went by, Jamie's spending habits caused him to lose trust and faith in her, and fights ensued. Despite their rocky relationship, Jamie was stunned when her husband left. At 32, she was abandoned with two small children. She needed to work to support them, and she had no outlet for her pain except shopping.

Withholding Father/Overprotective Mother

Olivia's father was one of the multitudes who disembarked from the commuter train every evening at 6:30. His job as an insurance salesman was a source of money—but not pride or satisfaction—and he never discussed work at home. Indeed, he rarely discussed much of anything at home. He would hastily eat dinner and retire to his easy chair in the den to read the newspaper. At 8:00 every night the television went on, and he watched it until 11:00. Then he went to bed. In the morning he was back on the commuter train before Olivia woke up.

Sometimes the silence in the house was punctuated by angry outbursts. One day her mother decided to make a special dinner. Olivia helped her prepare filet mignon with artichoke sauce and a lemon meringue pie. Olivia's father ate the entree without comment. By the time pie was served, Olivia's mother was seething.

Finally, she spoke up. "I don't know why I bother to make a nice dinner when you never notice. I slave at home and you—"

He stood up and threw his napkin down into the pie. "Slave? Who the hell gets up at 6:30 every morning and has to work all day?" he shouted, his face livid.

Olivia started crying. "Daddy, you ruined the pie and I helped make it."

"Nobody asked you, young lady. Now shut up!" he snapped.

She continued crying.

He yanked her up from her chair and shook her shoulders. "I said stop that crying. Shut up!"

Of course, this only made Olivia cry more hysterically. Finally, her father slapped her across the face and sent her up to her room. Later that night, her mother brought her a piece of the lemon meringue pie, but warned her not to tell her father.

"Nobody asked you" was one of his favorite comments. He would say it both to his wife and to Olivia when they expressed opinions. Olivia grew up feeling that she couldn't trust her feelings or thoughts, and that her opinions had no validity. In later years, when discussions arose, she would speak up combatively. She was so insecure about her opinions, afraid that people would judge her as wrong and bad, as her father had, that she needed to stridently cut down other people's ideas. A simple discussion often became a struggle, but it was actually fear of criticism and judgment that was behind her argumentative style.

To combat his surly silence, Olivia's mother would constantly nag her father. "You'll get into an accident if you don't put those snow tires on." "We could save some money on vegetables if you would help me with a garden." "Put your sweaty shirts in the hamper. I can't stand to pick them up off the floor." "The lawn will never grow in if you don't rake the leaves." And so on, season after season, year after year. Usually he would ignore her, sometimes he would grudgingly obey, and sometimes he would explode into fits of anger.

Olivia had to tread carefully around her father to avoid his explosions, and even then she couldn't always escape. She came to feel that the world was an unstable, unpredictable place. He displaced some of his anger toward his wife by picking on their daughter. Olivia was the middle child, and not only did her older sister and younger brother seem to conspire against her, her father did also.

"Like all little girls, I wanted to be a ballerina," Olivia remembered. "I was a little chubby, but I loved ballet class. I remember when my father came to my recital one year when I was nine. I ran up to him afterward, all excited in my little tutu, and I'll never forget what he said. He said, 'You look like a baby elephant. Your mother should stop giving you all that candy.' Well, of course, after that the dancing was ruined for me. I never went back to ballet school."

Olivia tried to win her father's approval by working diligently and doing well in grade school, but no matter how glowing her report cards were, he never seemed to notice. He noticed, however, if she did the slightest thing wrong, like leaving the telephone off the hook or leaving her room even slightly untidy. One of his favorite phrases was, "Can't you do anything right?"

Olivia's mother, on the other hand, smothered her. She paid cloying attention to her every activity and was quite overprotective. Although she didn't actually prohibit Olivia from doing things, she created a climate of fear. She would say, "It's dangerous sleigh-riding on that hill," or "You could get hit by a car bike-riding on that busy street." This added to Olivia's sense of the world as a dangerous place. Her mother imbued every separation with anxiety, leading to Olivia's grown-up dependence on her husband and inability to be comfortable alone.

When Olivia reached adolescence, her father had a difficult time with his feelings of sexuality toward her, and he became even more critical and mocking. "My mother got me my own phone when I was 15, and I used to spend hours on it with my girlfriends. Sometimes my father would overhear me talking about boyfriends and he would make fun of me. I was so humiliated and embarrassed," said Olivia. He also added to the insecurity that all teen-agers feel by criticizing her clothes, her hairstyles and her boyfriends.

One way that Olivia and her mother could have some fun away from the pressures of home was to go shopping. Early on, shopping became a form of escape and release. Olivia's mother would buy her things, and they would often hide them in the trunk of the car until her father was at work the next day. "My father always begrudged everything she bought me, said I didn't need it. So we just wouldn't let him know." When asked how much a purchase cost, they often lied about the true price out of fear of his volatile reactions.

Immediately after college, Olivia married Frank, the first man with whom she had a serious relationship. Although kind and well-meaning, Frank found it as difficult to understand and express his feelings as Olivia did. During the course of their marriage, neither partner truly communicated with the other when issues arose. She would vent her frustration by nagging at her husband and children about little things—and by going shopping.

Sexually Abused Child

Lisa M. grew up in a middle-class home that seethed with hostility underneath its "normal" facade. Her father, a postal supervisor, was a tyrannical man who completely dominated his timid wife. "I always knew how my father's work was going, not because he talked about it, but because if things were going badly he'd pick on us." said Lisa. He was bitter about life and wanted more, so he took it out on his family. Lisa and her mother were often nervous before her father came home from work, never knowing from one day to the next what his mood would be. Would this be another night of fighting, during which he became verbally abusive? Sometimes his body language and the look on his face alone were enough to create a joyless atmosphere.

Her mother was a full-time housewife who loved gardening. However, her husband would comment only on the imperfections in the color and size of the fresh vegetables she served, demeaning one of her only sources of pride. He would also complain that she spent too much time "fussing with those stupid weeds."

One evening Lisa's mother failed to have dinner ready when her husband came home from work because she was absorbed in her gardening. When he saw her in the garden instead of the kitchen, he became enraged. "You care more about those weeds than your own husband!" he shouted. He began to stomp and thrash around the garden, ruining many of the blooms.

Lisa grew up intimidated by her father and identifying with her weak, timid mother. She felt she had no one to turn to when things went wrong. "In second grade there was a group of girls who made me their scapegoat, I think because I wore thick glasses. They'd call me all kinds of names and be really cruel. I was miserable, but I had to keep it inside. I felt that I couldn't tell my father; he was even meaner than the girls. And it seemed hopeless to tell my mother. She couldn't stand up for herself, so how could she help me?"

Soon Lisa had a much more shameful secret to keep from her

parents. Around the time she was eight or nine years old—Lisa has blocked out the exact age—an older teen-age cousin was left to babysit with her. Lisa vividly recalls the three episodes, which still make her shiver with disgust and revulsion.

Her cousin would come into her bedroom when she was reading in bed. He would lift up her nightgown and fondle her. He said that he was doing nice things, but she mustn't tell anyone about them, or she would get into trouble. Lisa knew it wasn't "nice," that it was very bad indeed. However, she was far too humiliated and fearful to tell her father about it. She also felt that her mother was too weak and ineffectual to help. So she let the secret fester inside her, hiding the three episodes from both her parents and husband.

Keeping this type of secret is very unhealthy, making a person emotionally repressed and unable to let go of the pain. It also prevents a person from feeling wholly and truly loved. Somewhere deep inside, Lisa feared that if anyone knew her dirty secret, they wouldn't love her anymore. As she grew older, she felt unworthy of the love of a good man and terrified that if she found one, he would leave her if he knew.

Lisa not only felt powerless and humiliated after her molestation, she also felt guilty. Most children believe the reason other people do things is because of something they themselves have done. Therefore, the victim's feeling of culpability is inherent in child abuse. The victims do not simply blame the molestor; they blame themselves.

Lisa turned her anger at her father and her cousin on herself and grew up with very low self-esteem. Basically terrified of men, she stuck with her first high school boyfriend even though he showed some characteristics similar to her father. After they were married, Kevin's domineering nature surfaced in full force. Lisa adopted the model of her submissive mother, expressing her rebellion only through her shopping habits. She went shopping to escape from her inner torment and rage. On an unconscious level she was terrified of her murderous rage. The male role models from her childhood were hardly safe, loving or nurturing. This caused her to feel unsafe, always on the brink of being abandoned. Because of this, she had to be the "good girl" with her friends and her husband. She never took the risk of being herself and finding out that she was worthy of love.

There is a high correlation between sexual abuse and compulsive shopping. In my treatment of addicted spenders, there has been an unusually high percentage of women who have been abused either by a parent or relative. It should be noted that although we have no true statistics on the extent of this problem, we do know that it occurs in families of every race, creed and socioeconomic class. Professional help is necessary to deal with this devastating experience. If you have suffered from sexual abuse, it is advisable that you see a professional therapist or join one of the groups that addresses this serious problem.

Loss of Mother

When Richard N. was five years old, his mother died in a car accident. He remembers the funeral, seeing his father and all the other relatives cry. He also remembers asking over and over again, "Where's Mommy? When's Mommy coming back?" Although he had been told that she was dead, it was beyond his comprehension that she could really be gone forever, that she had abandoned him.

When young children lose their parents they feel many emotions in addition to sorrow. Children often believe they are responsible for their parents' "disappearance," creating a feeling of guilt and confusion. If children who lose their parents ever had a momentary wish that their parents would disappear or die, their guilt can become unbearable.

Children also feel anger and confusion at being abandoned when they lose a parent. "How could you forsake me?" they wonder. Yet, while this question burns inside them, they often can't allow themselves to consciously express this anger. After all, how can they be angry at a dead parent? So the anger is turned inward, where it fosters the growth of self-hatred and worthlessness. They grow up with a core of sadness, feeling they weren't worthy enough for their parents to stay. The world becomes a frightening and unpredictable place. If mother can suddenly disappear, anything can happen at any time. They can count on nothing. Children feel powerless in this frightening and indifferent universe.

However, if a child's remaining parent is supportive and loving, allowing the child to express his or her feelings and work through the trauma, the child will learn to adapt and will not suffer serious loss of self-esteem. This was not the case with Richard.

Richard suffered a great deal over the loss of his mother. He never had anyone with whom he could talk and share his feelings of confusion and pain. There was a series of female relatives who helped out when he was young, but they were too preoccupied with their own families to pay enough attention to him. His father was an inarticulate, simple man, well-meaning but totally unequipped to deal with the complexities of his own feelings, let alone his son's.

"Every night it went the same way," recalled Richard. "My father and I would sit across from each other at the dinner table and he'd say, 'How was school today?' without even looking up from his plate. I'd say 'okay,' and he'd say, 'Make sure you do all your homework before you watch any more TV,' and I'd say 'okay.' That would be it. Sometimes I would start to tell him how school really was, but he never seemed to know what to say. He'd listen, say a few pat things and keep eating. So I gave up trying to talk to him. What was the use?"

Richard would think other mothers looked so nice when they came to school and when he went to visit his friends' houses. As the memories of his own mother began to fade, he started creating a fantasy: a mother who was beautiful, kind, nurturing and always there for him. He spent hours on end imagining all the things he and his fantasy mother would do together. He learned to create an imaginary world instead of expressing his feelings and trying to get what he needed from the real world.

It was quite natural that he would become a comic book fanatic. Comics offered an absorbing alternative universe that distracted him from the emptiness of his own. They depicted heroes who were wonderfully powerful and could save lovely women from certain death, unlike his father and he, who had done nothing to save his mother. And what had his father done to save him from feeling all alone?

Comic books also gave him his first taste of personal power. He began to trade them with other boys, then buy more with the money he made. This gave him an intoxicating sense of control and mastery over the boys who coveted his comics. It also made him feel different from his father, whom he increasingly viewed as ineffectual and weak.

One day when he was ten years old, the class was given an assignment to write about their fathers' work. Richard went to visit his father at his bookkeeping job. "The boss treated him like dirt, criticizing his work right in front of me," Richard remembered. "My father just took it, nodding obediently and continuing to work like a robot. I was so humiliated for him. I was also mad at him for being like that."

Richard was mad at his mother for dying and at his father for being ineffectual. This anger was repressed and turned inward, creating self-doubt and low self-esteem—common seeds for compulsion.

The seeds blossomed when he was 18. His aunt gave him a camera for high school graduation which he took on a camping trip that summer. Several of the boys took their girlfriends along on the trip, but Richard never had a girl.

One of the guys brought his girlfriend Deirdre, a beautiful blonde whom Richard often fantasized about. She was everything Richard and his father were not: bold, self-confident, spontaneous and joyful.

"Let me borrow your camera so I can take some pictures of Deirdre sunbathing," Jonathan asked Richard. He hesitated. Jonathan had the girl he wanted, but Richard had the camera. This gave him a feeling of power that somewhat compensated for his loneliness and jealousy.

"If you want to use it, you have to buy it," Richard said.

"How much?"

"Fifty bucks."

"It's not worth that. It's just a crummy Instamatic."

"You don't want it, you don't get any pictures of Deirdre."

Jonathan dug into his pocket and fished out fifty dollars to buy Richard's camera.

That night, as Richard lay in his tent alone, knowing that there were couples nearby, he consoled himself thinking of the money he had coerced from Jonathan. He couldn't win the girl, but he had won the barter. He thought about buying a better camera as soon as he got home and later selling or trading it. Richard was well on his way toward an adult obsession with buying and selling camera equipment, a compulsion that masqueraded as a "hobby" but was really an outlet for his anger, his insecurity and his need for control.

Restrictive, Joyless Home Life

When David decided to risk getting into his own business instead of taking a safe, salaried job, he thought he was overcoming the legacy of his parents. He took chances. But his inability to save or invest money revealed that he still suffered from the effects of his upbringing.

David's parents had grown up during the Depression, and its memory had made them financially conservative in their later years. His father worked as a middle manager in the same corporation for 42 years. "If he had put that kind of time and effort into his own business, he could have really made out, but he was afraid to risk it," said David.

His parents were also afraid to enjoy the money they had. Purchases for the house and the children were carefully discussed; there was no spontaneous buying. They never took vacations and rarely spent money on entertainment. "Thinking back, I wonder if my parents had any fun at all. They didn't have any special hobbies, didn't do any sports, didn't go to movies, and I don't remember anyone coming to our home. I don't even remember them laughing."

Many compulsive shoppers come from homes where life is skeletal—composed of doing one's work and duty and little else. Parents who are frightened of expanding their world create a constricted environment. Their children lack the experience and imagination to enjoy a variety of activities in life. The dearth of internal resources, combined with the influence of the media in promoting the message that shopping is pleasurable and satisfying, turns many of these children into shopping addicts. Like their parents before them, they too may live limited, joyless lives.

David moved far away from his parents, thinking that would ensure a true separation. His socially hectic lifestyle masked the joylessness he felt inside. David would congratulate himself for being so different from his parents. He felt compelled to maintain this difference by spending recklessly. This made him feel free from their constricted, limited world. But no one is really free if they are a slave to a shopping addiction.

David liked to think of himself as an independent man, fully separated from his parents. But having no money in the bank for emergencies implied that someone—his parents most likely—might have to bail him out someday. Developmentally, he was not totally beyond the stage of dependency on his parents. This behavior pattern is often an unconscious process among compulsive shoppers. They are not aware of the connection between their shopping habits and their desire to be taken care of in a way they were not as children.

Addicted Parent

"I never thought of my mother as a pill addict," said Anne. "After all, she was a respectable mother and housewife. But I did know that she couldn't do without her tranquilizers. When she tried to give them up, she became an absolute wreck. My father never encouraged her to stop taking pills. I guess he liked the way they kept her quiet and docile. In fact, I bet she originally got the prescription because he made her so nervous."

Like many compulsive people, Anne's mother manifested more than one addiction. "My mother smoked two packs of cigarettes a day. When all the anti-smoking propaganda came out, I got really worried about her. Once I saw a program in school about how dangerous cigarettes were. When I got home, I started crying and begged her to stop. She said she would, and I guess she tried, but in a day or so the ashtrays were full again. It didn't give me much faith in people's ability to break bad habits."

Children learn many behaviors from their parents, from basics such as walking and talking to complex patterns of social interaction. They also can model the compulsive behavior that leads to full-fledged addiction. Children universally imitate their parents, which can result in addictions that are passed from one generation to another.

Parents of compulsive shoppers do not necessarily have spending addictions, although this sometimes occurs. They may have been drug abusers, chronic gamblers, or had more socially acceptable addictions to food, caffeine and/or cigarettes.

Many shopping addicts had parents who suffered from alcoholism, a prevalent and disastrous disease. Alcoholics are often volatile and moody, creating chaos and fear in their households. Their children grow up feeling that the world is an unpredictable and potentially hostile place.

To make matters worse, the spouses of alcoholics often develop addictions of their own in an attempt to dull the pain of their marriages. This model for coping, coupled with the shame and insecurity caused by the alcoholic parent, makes the children vulnerable to addiction. Even if they don't turn to alcohol, they are likely to turn to another form of addictive behavior, such as compulsive shopping.

Economic and Emotional Deprivation

All the cases discussed in this chapter involve middle-class families, but compulsive spenders can come from any background—rich or poor.

Although poverty itself does not necessarily lead to compulsive shopping, poverty is often accompanied by feelings of hopelessness, resignation, frustration and despair. It is very difficult for parents who have these feelings to take time to enjoy their children and provide a healthy, nurturing atmosphere. So often the children are hit with a double whammy: they lack both the things money can buy and the things money can't buy. This double deprivation often spawns addiction.

If parents create a loving, joyful environment, regardless of how much money they do or do not have, their children will most likely grow up with responsible spending habits. But if there is emotional deprivation, people from poor homes can become overspenders. •

I get a real thrill
out of wining and
dining gorgeous
ladies, even though
I can't afford it. I
just can't resist.
—David

Chapter 3

The Nature of Addiction

The first step toward recovery from a compulsive shopping habit is to recognize that shopping can be a serious addiction. It is often difficult for people to accept this concept, because shopping is something that everyone does. However, you might consider this. Everyone eats, yet compulsive overeating is recognized as an addiction. Many people have an alcoholic beverage now and then, but compulsive drinking leads to alcoholism. Addictions do not always endanger physical aspects of health, but they always have a severely detrimental effect on psychological health.

There are two main categories of addiction: substance abuse and addictive behavior. Behavioral addictions can be attached to almost anything: sex, gambling, work, television, exercising, and of course, shopping. None of these activities is inherently dangerous or destructive. It is only when they begin to interfere with other aspects of life that they become a problem. When the behavior begins to take control—causing the person to act inappropriately, deny and try to escape from problems, and go against personal values—it should be considered an addiction.

When confronted with the idea that shopping is an addiction, many compulsive spenders react with denial. Even those who admit to the problem often resist seeking help. They are typically upstanding members of the community and do not want to be associated with an alcoholic lying in a doorway or a junkie in a shooting gallery. Granted, there is a difference, in that the junkie or alcoholic often ceases to function in and contribute to society. This is the opposite of compulsive shoppers whom I treat, who usually contribute a great deal to society.

A defensive posture only serves to keep the shopping addict from admitting the impact of his or her compulsion and seeking help. It stands in the way of progress and recovery. It is based on the false assumption that being addicted means a person is bad, worthless and destructive to society. Many addicted people are destructive only to themselves and sometimes to their loved ones.

Certain characteristics are shared by most addictive personalities. This chapter will address these qualities in general, and also discuss how they are manifested specifically in compulsive shopping. This should make clear that compulsive shopping can be an addiction that demands recognition and treatment.

Failed Standards of Perfection

Many addictive people are among those with the highest standards and aspirations. They have unrealistically grand expectations of themselves. When they don't live up to them, they plunge into despair. They cannot forgive themselves for being flawed and imperfect, as all of us are, so they drown their disappointment in addiction.

Often the parents of compulsive shoppers have an illusion of the "perfect child" and instill these unrealistic expectations into their offspring during their upbringing. To compensate for their own self-doubts, these parents see everything in terms of black and white, good and bad. What follows is a child, and later an adult, who feels branded as a failure. This situation can also create a primary addiction: the addiction to perfection.

"No matter how hard I tried, it seemed I was never good enough for my mother," said Jamie. "If I got seven A's and one B on my report card, she'd remark on the B. She'd say something like, 'You'll never get a scholarship if you don't get top marks, and we can't afford to pay for your college.' That made both my father and me feel like failures in one fell swoop."

Jamie's father, however, would not only lavishly praise her achievements, he would also buy her something as a reward. However, pretty things could never make up for the feeling that she had failed her mother. She was never good enough. How could she be?

Children who grow up with parents who set impossible standards for them become hooked on performance and self-packaging. They lose their natural spontaneity in a rush to attain and achieve. This leads to a level of pressure that needs an outlet. That outlet is often an addiction of one sort or another.

Many addictive personalities not only have great expectations of themselves, they also have them of others. When others disappoint them, it increases the bitterness and sense of betrayal they already feel. Jamie expected her husband to be the perfect lover, father and provider all in one, offering an everflowing abundance of unconditional love. When he failed to live up to her ideal and manifested human flaws, their marriage broke up.

The ancient Greeks had a word to describe the tragic flaw of their mythological heroes: *hubris,* meaning an excessive amount of pride. This is the downfall of many modern men and women as well. It is linked to an idealized self that recognizes no human limitations. The flip side of this coin is inevitably the low self-esteem that results from the failure to constantly live up to this ideal.

We often turn to addictive behavior because we are at war with ourselves. Whether it's drugs or shopping, the addiction serves as an opiate to dull the pain of the wounds suffered in this inner civil war. But there is another, much healthier solution.

We can make peace with ourselves by accepting our flaws, our limitations, our defects. We should not only accept them, we should love them! Remember they are what make us living, feeling human beings. Everyone agrees it is virtuous to be kind, easygoing and forgiving with others. However, in order to be sincerely tolerant and accepting of others, it is necessary that we cultivate genuine self-love and self-acceptance. We should learn to love ourselves and be happy and peaceful, even when we do things that are "wrong." Castigating ourselves only results in more pain; it won't erase limitations or disappointments. On the contrary, not loving ourselves and being gentle with ourselves when we are most flawed or vulnerable only perpetuates our behavior. Loving ourselves with our imperfections frees us to be the best we can—and that is always "right."

The ability to free ourselves from self-criticism and nurture ourselves in any condition or circumstance has a wonderful side effect: it allows us to be open to others and truly love them for who they are. It is virtually impossible to be an emotional victim in the world when acceptance is the major theme in one's life.

Seeking Control, Living in Chaos

When parents fail to give their children an inner sense of security, they develop a great need for control over their actions and their environment. They become locked into rigid patterns of behavior in order to obtain a false sense of security. Life becomes an automatic series of responses instead of spontaneous, free-flowing experiences.

Needing to be in control is actually a manifestation of deeply felt insecurity and anxiety. Buying cameras and reselling them at a higher price gave Richard a feeling of control over others. He loved making a profit and getting better and newer equipment. He needed this sense of control to compensate for the helplessness he felt because of his mother's death and his father's weakness.

Richard was an anxiety-ridden person who had never resolved his parental issues. His need for control was great, but that type of compulsion begs for release. The "highs" of his camera "wheeling and dealing" provided this release, so buying and selling took precedence over all other aspects of his life. This locked him into a narrow world.

The need to control leads to a great deal of suffering. People try to control because they are fearful of the world in general and change in particular. Controlling personalities are susceptible to addictions because they so desperately need release from fear and anxiety. They lack faith that they can be the architects of their lives, with legitimate control over their destinies. Instead of allowing themselves healthy and appropriate freedom, they lose themselves in addiction. In Latin, the word "addiction" comes from the word "surrender." When an addiction is formed, compulsive shoppers surrender their internal power and give themselves up to shopping. The addiction creates chaos in their lives, leading to a greater yearning for control. This exacerbates the desire for release through shopping, so another downward spiral of addiction results.

To be a relaxed person and live a free and happy life, it is important to learn to let go, to relinquish control when appropriate. In order to feel secure, it is necessary to perceive the world as basically safe and sympathetic, not hostile. This is difficult because of the constant stream of news about violence. Remember that violence is news because it is *outside the norm,* and it doesn't have to infringe on our world view. We can create as much peace or strife as we choose in our own worlds and within our own homes.

Once we can let go of internal fears, the need to control is no longer paramount. We feel safer than ever because we are more in touch with the natural rhythms of the world and ourselves. No one can fully control himself, others or the environment. Trying to do so only results in constriction and pain. Letting go of control results in a fuller, more expansive life.

Trying to maintain tight control also limits growth. Growth and change can be painful, which is why many people try to resist them. But they are inevitable and integral parts of life, without which one stagnates and eventually experiences either spiritual or physical death.

Clinging to an addictive behavior can be an effort to maintain stasis, to keep things as they are. Buddhist philosophy states that all human suffering stems from an attempt to resist change in a universe that is constantly in flux. We can all learn from this: it is vital to accept the ebb and flow of life. Acceptance of this philosophy is not easy and initially can inspire fear. However, if we can learn to live moment by moment, attempting to make the everyday special, our lives will be greatly enhanced. This attitude develops inner strength and resources, and a wellspring of inner resources eliminates the need for addiction.

When we do something long enough, we often begin to believe on a subconscious level that we must keep doing it in order to survive—even if we consciously acknowledge that it is destructive behavior. These negative thought patterns can be as addictive as any drug. However, they can be changed by employing affirmations and other techniques that will be discussed in depth in the latter part of this book. Once you stop clinging to the belief that the past inevitably shapes your present and future, negativity loses its power. You can dump the garbage of the past and begin to take the necessary steps to create the life you want for yourself.

Dependency

Dependent personalities develop when parents fail to make their children feel safe and secure during the separation process. When these children mature, they may become dependent on other people to make decisions for them and take care of them because they fear standing on their own. These people have a predisposition toward compulsive and addictive behavior. Addicted people depend on their habit to relieve tension and provide an escape from problems they don't want to face.

Dependency needs can be overt or subtle. Many compulsive shoppers cling to others, while some pretend they need no one. Regardless of the particular stance that shopping addicts project, they harbor grave doubts regarding their self-reliance and self-esteem. Deep down, they still feel like helpless children who need someone to depend on. If they turn to people who deeply love them, they often find fault or deficiency in this love. They devalue the person who loves them because they don't feel deserving of that love. How could anyone of any true value love them? The addiction substitutes for the unconditional love of the parent/caretaker. At this point the thought of an equal partnership may be threatening, but as the addiction is shed the possibilities for true partnership increase.

Denial and Avoidance

Just as many addictive personalities deny their dependency needs, they also deny anger, fear and other negative emotions. Lisa denied her outrage at the incidents of molestation in her youth, telling herself that she had gotten over them a long time ago. But having never gotten in touch fully with her rage and guilt, she had not truly recovered. Because the anger had not been released, it festered inside and resulted in shopping binges as a form of self-punishment and revenge.

By not honoring her struggle and pain, Lisa denied not only her anger, but her very being. To honor yourself means respecting and dealing with both the good and bad events in your life. Only if you acknowledge them can you master the traumas you have suffered. Denial lends them more power.

Compulsive activities are often used to fill empty, quiet moments and avoid making contact with the inner self. The addictive behavior is an attempt to avoid experiencing what is occurring in one's mind and soul. "When I go shopping, I forget about everything that's bothering me," is a statement made by many compulsive shoppers in group sessions. By becoming absorbed in the addictive behavior, people reach an almost hypnotic state. This diverts them from the things they are denying, the things that make them uncomfortable. This numbed consciousness also prevents them from taking in life fully.

Support groups are very important in dealing with addictions, because once the addictive behavior is stopped, many distressing thoughts reach consciousness. The mind is somewhat like a pool that has been neglected for a long time; the debris must be cleared away before you can enjoy swimming in it. This process can be unpleasant, but that is temporary and certainly preferable to addiction. Once the denied experiences and feelings are dealt with, one can experience life in a more whole, vibrant and fully awake manner than ever before.

Deception and Shame

Denial is a means by which people deceive themselves. Once self-deception is mastered, a person can easily deceive others, especially if he or she is ashamed of an addiction. This dishonesty leads to greater shame and negative feelings.

Compulsive shoppers hide purchases like alcoholics hide bottles. Many addicted spenders stuff clothing behind other outfits in their closets in order to hide it from their spouses. They also develop other tricks of deception. "Sometimes, I'll wear something I got during a shopping binge and Jeff will say, 'You went out and bought another new dress?' in an accusing kind of way. And I'll say something like, 'I've had this dress for years, but you never remember what I wear anyhow,'" said Anne. "That gets him all confused. He doesn't know what's new or what's old or how much I'm spending. I can't honestly say I feel good about lying to Jeff, but I feel so ashamed and nervous, I don't know what else to do." Another thing that Anne and many compulsive shoppers routinely do is lie about prices, making the purchases sound like irresistible bargains. This deception also leads to more shame and less self-respect.

Compulsive shoppers also deceive others by acting as if they have more money than they do. David, with his extravagant entertaining, was a prime example of this. He was afraid that he would not be respected for who he was, so he needed to present a false image. In this way, he closed himself off from being loved and accepted for his essence.

One Friday after work David met three friends at a popular restaurant. When the bill came, David did the usual; he dipped into his wall for his credit card and paid the bill. His friends, accustomed to David's insistence about paying, didn't even bother to offer to share the tab. Later that evening, David began to question the motives behind his "generosity." He started to feel queasy, as if he were being taken advantage of, yet he knew he created these situations. Instead of getting upset at his friends, he turned the anger inward and became depressed.

Deception not only produces shame and guilt, it also weakens relationships. It keeps people from feeling that they can be truly loved and accepted for who they are. It's inevitable that when you're not true to yourself, relationships with others will be confused and unsatisfying. People often lie to avoid confrontations, but when the truth emerges, it causes more serious confrontations. Everything backfires. Addicted people lie because they don't want to be discovered and be forced to face their addictions or be deprived of them. They also don't want to face what the addictions are masking.

Honesty is essential for recovery from addiction. First, you must admit the problem to yourself, then to your loved ones and to any others in your support network. This takes courage, but it reaps enormous benefits. You will no longer feel helplessly alone with your problem, and you will eliminate a source of shame and guilt. Also, you will probably be surprised and relieved by the support and acceptance you receive from others when you bring your shopping problem "out of the closet." People will applaud you for your honesty and courage, and be willing to help.

Depression

Depression has reached epidemic proportions in our society and leads many people into addiction. Depressive states vary widely in frequency, duration and intensity, ranging from a momentary feeling to a chronic state that requires hospitalization. Some of the characteristics of severe depression are: a change in eating habits, sleeping disturbances, loss of sexual interest, lethargy, inability to function, irritability, and a general loss of enthusiasm about life.

If a person feels that his depression is chronic—as opposed to reactive depression, which is triggered by specific events, such as loss of a loved one—he should see a doctor. There are biological as well as psychological reasons for depression. Also, remaining depressed for long periods of time is very unhealthy. If a person has tried independent means of eliminating depression and nothing has worked, professional help should be sought.

People who suffer from regular bouts of depression are often dependent personalities; when life becomes difficult, they are likely to turn to addiction. They may turn to drugs and/or compulsive activity. They depend on the addiction to give them a momentary lift out of the depressive state. "Sometimes it's so hard to get out of bed in the morning," said Jamie. "I just want to pull the quilt over my head and forget about it all—work, the kids, everything. I know I have to get up and drag myself through the day, so I have a little trick: I tell myself that I can go shopping if I do everything else I have to do. I think about something nice for the house that I can buy, and that gets me up and going."

Jamie, like many compulsive shoppers, has suffered from undiagnosed mild depression since her childhood. Shopping was one of the only activities that induced a break from the weight of her mood. However, as with drugs or alcohol, a crash inevitably occurred after the binge, and the waves of depression would start rolling in again.

Most compulsive shoppers who suffer from depression do not go shopping until they are beginning to move out of the depressive state. It is then that they have enough energy to mobilize themselves to go shopping, rationalizing that they have suffered so much they deserve to spend. This emergence from depression is an important time for compulsive spenders to recognize their feelings of entitlement—which can lead to a binge—and postpone shopping. It is much safer and wiser to wait until the mood of well-being has stabilized and feels genuine before going shopping.

Spiritual Bankruptcy

Like depression, addiction is rampant in our modern world. There is a great deal of public funding and attention devoted to the treatment of substance abuse. Also, individuals spend millions of their own dollars seeking cures for alcoholism, drug addiction and eating disorders. However, little effort or funding is directed toward the study of behavioral addictions such as compulsive shopping. Therefore, people are much less likely to actively seek treatment. This may be because the effects of behavioral addictions are more insidious. Although they can destroy the spirit, they usually do not destroy the body. In this society, the body is often slavishly cared for while the spirit languishes in neglect.

It is not surprising that Alcoholics Anonymous, the most successful organization in the world for treating alcoholism, has a religious basis for its recovery program. A.A. meetings begin with the serenity prayer: *God grant me the serenity to accept the things I cannot change, the courage to change the things I can and the wisdom to know the difference.* The famous "Twelve Steps" of A.A. involve surrendering to God and praying for help to conquer alcoholism. Perhaps one of the reasons this program is so successful is that drinking, as with other addictions, is often a false way to achieve transcendence. A synonym for alcohol is "spirits," and people get "high" on drugs.

Compulsive shoppers experience a "high" when in the stores. The addiction can be a way to escape the mundane world and experience an almost mystical state of rapture, similar to that which is felt during religious ecstasy. However, the addicts' ecstasy is a false and unsatisfying one: they are always left lower than before, thereby craving more of the addictive substance or behavior.

There is yet another way that addiction substitutes for spirituality. People have a deep-rooted need for ritual, and addictions can take on a ritualistic aspect. For an alcoholic it may be buying his favorite liquor, perhaps at a particular time of the day, in a certain bar, day in and day out, imbibing and feeling the warm glow. For the compulsive spender the ritual may involve gathering the credit cards and money and making the pilgrimage to the stores. An added aspect of the shopping ritual for some is the meeting of friends on a regular basis. Instead of meeting in church, synagogue or the town square, they meet at the mall to get their sustenance. These rituals are comforting constants in a world that is changing too quickly. However, they are perverted rituals in the sense that they bring the participant further into unconsciousness, instead of into a truly expanded state.

People with addictive personalities often have a greater than ordinary need and capacity for spirituality. Once they begin to deal with their problems and free themselves from addiction, this spiritual aspect can become a wonderful tool toward building a creative life.

It is important for everyone, but especially for potentially addictive personalities, to pay attention to their spiritual needs. This may mean becoming involved in an organized religion, or it may mean cultivating the spiritual aspects of your inner being. There are many paths that lead to the same place. Whatever road is comfortable and feels right is the one to follow.

The Need for Heroes

The Greek myths and even older oral traditions of ancient cultures attest to the universal need for heroes. But in our society, instead of genuine, deserving, lasting heroes, we have superficial idols created by the entertainment and news media. By exposing the corruption or peccadillos of public figures, the news media destroy idols almost as quickly as they create them.

The entertainment media often encourage us to worship those who are wealthy and/or have alluring images, instead of people who do important and substantial work. This image worship promotes compulsive shopping. People keep buying and buying in order to look more like the rich and beautiful people they wish to emulate. They feel that if only they keep spending, they'll be like their heroes. Yet, on some level, they know there is something more. This fuels their despair and the need to escape through addiction.

The Breakdown of Family and Community

There are now approximately 5 billion people on the earth, yet many people feel more alone than ever. We are a "global village" without a sense of family or community identity.

Until very recently, most people remained in or near the community where they grew up. The entire community was, in a sense, their family. Often people shared dwellings with extended family members—parents, children, grandchildren and siblings all under one roof. This cushioned people from the unpredictability of life.

Now the cushions have been pulled out from under many of us. Extended families rarely live in the same dwelling, and often live very far apart. Upward mobility can entail leaving one's relatives and old friends far behind. Even the nuclear family unit has been blown apart by divorce. Although the divorce rate is now going down, we are still feeling aftershocks of the soaring rates of the last two decades.

Loneliness is probably the most widespread and infrequently addressed problem of our society. Many city dwellers live in buildings with people they never meet. For many others, the telephone is the only connection with loved ones. Even for those with families and many friends, the lack of community ties can lead to a feeling of isolation.

If loneliness is not a problem, finding one's place in society may be. It is wonderful that we now have so many choices about what roles to play in the world, but it can also be frightening and confusing. Now we must travel life's road without a map. This makes it tempting to pull off the road and take a detour into an addiction.

"Where do I fit in?" and "What is the meaning of my life?" are questions that plague more people than ever before. Tackling these problems alone, without a strong support system, is difficult at best. At worst, it can lead to despair, which makes escape into an addiction very seductive.

You don't have to be without a roof to feel like a homeless person. In order to feel truly at home in the world, it is necessary to have more than food, clothing and shelter. One must also have food for the soul. Addicted people are often unable to take a sincere look at their needs. They aspire to a quality life, but on some level don't believe it's possible. So they numb themselves into unconsciousness, becoming metaphorically homeless—not at home in their body, mind or spirit.

The Advertising Message

The lack of spirituality and absence of worthy role models, coupled with the breakdown of the extended family and community, creates a void in many souls. Into this emptiness is poured an unceasing advertising message: buy, buy, buy!

Many children grow up with television as a babysitter, the electronic images replacing the constant attention of a loving mother. They are weaned on a diet of seductive television commercials instead of deep values. It is no wonder that shopping addictions are on the rise.

Television, radio, magazines, newspapers—all of the media that play such an important part in our consciousness—are strewn with enticing advertisements. We are not being persuaded to buy merely objects—we are being sold a way of being. The subliminal message is that if we buy a certain perfume, we'll be as sexy as the model wearing it. If we buy a certain dress, we'll be chic and thin. If we buy a certain liquor, we'll have dazzling parties. If we buy, we'll be whatever we want to be—young, beautiful, rich, successful, happy.

This powerful message is presented in creative and inventive ways. Talented professionals create advertising campaigns that convince millions of people they want something they don't need. It is no coincidence that they are called advertising "campaigns"—they are conducted with all the vigor, enthusiasm and financial backing devoted to political and military campaigns. And they are often much more successful.

The models are gorgeous, the settings imaginative, the words carefully chosen to evoke the right response. Even the psychological effect of colors is utilized. Then the advertisements are displayed relentlessly to a population starved for the nourishment of lasting values and relationships. Almost everyone is somewhat affected. Statistics show that consumer buying has escalated by staggering degrees. It is difficult for anyone to avoid accepting at least some of the advertising messages. For impressionable addictive personalities, the messages can be lethal.

Spending: A Form of Worship

Many people today are not conscious of the fact that fulfillment comes not just from making money, but from accomplishment. This attitude can lead to misplaced values and confusion. The dollar is often worshipped for its own sake, so people want to appear rich even when they are not—so they overspend.

Spending money is an inalienable right in our free-enterprise society. Indeed, it is often confused with that other right, the pursuit of happiness. There will never be laws to curb spending, nor should there be. Compulsive shoppers will never be able to avoid stores, advertisements and other inducements to spend. The regulations will never come from the outside. They must come from within. Free enterprise demands that people develop responsible spending habits, or get sucked into the whirlpool of compulsive shopping.

Triumph Over Addiction

If you are now convinced that shopping is a serious addiction and you suffer from it, this means you are already on the road to recovery. Acknowledging a problem and seeking help is the first—and often most difficult—step. Reaching out requires courage and self-respect. This is the beginning of understanding and treating yourself in a loving, accepting way.

A prerequisite for overcoming addiction is meeting yourself with gentleness and hope. Then you can be fully awakened to who you are and what you need, acknowledging and accepting both your strengths and problems. With honesty and love, you can give and receive according to your true needs. You can feel at home and at one with the universe at large and with your inner being. •

When I purchase elegant clothing, I can pretend to be one of the beautiful people.

—Claudia R.

Chapter 4

Buying Self-Esteem, Power, Image and Love

Claudia R. wore her black hair pulled back and secured in a neat French knot at the nape of her long neck. This sleek hairstyle drew attention to her prominent cheekbones, large dark eyes and generous lips. Her tall, trim body was clothed in a salmon pink linen suit that complemented the light-coffee tone of her skin. From her pedicured toenails peeking out from open-toed Chanel pumps to her cultured-pearl earrings, she was the picture of tasteful elegance.

It was a picture Claudia paid a high price to paint. She spent approximately $7,000 a month on her wardrobe and accessories. Her bills for hairdressers and manicurists ran about $250 a month. Her job as the director of telecommunications for a large investment company earned her a good yearly salary of $50,000, but it was not nearly enough to cover her lavish expenditures.

Claudia was obsessively committed to fulfilling other peoples' expectations. She had grown to feel that these expectations included her maintenance of an impressive image. Because she lacked self-esteem, she became addicted to the compliments her appearance elicited from both men and women. Never feeling truly confident within, she relied on outside approval.

"Everything I buy has to say 'Claudia' on it," she said. Her perfectionism, stemming from a deep sense of insecurity, required that everything she buy be exceptional, not in the least ordinary. She shopped only in the most expensive stores, buying only exquisite items. Her purchases went far beyond her true needs. They included such extravagances as: three winter white Adolfo suits; seven silk blouses in beige hues; twelve couture evening dresses, including an Oscar de la Renta gown that cost $7,500; eight pairs of Ralph Lauren slacks; six Italian black leather handbags; and nine pairs of Chanel pumps.

Compulsive shoppers like Claudia rarely buy items they need. Instead, they purchase things that reflect qualities they feel they lack: self-esteem, love, power and/or a satisfying image. Healthy self-esteem involves self-love, self-respect and self-acceptance. When you feel a sense of appropriate control and effectiveness in the world, your image reflects and pleases your inner self.

Many people like to play with their images, creating different "looks" for different occasions. A woman might create a glamorous look for a special evening, and a casual look for a sunny afternoon. However, when image takes on a persona of its own to compensate for feelings of worthlessness, this game becomes dangerous. An obsession with image can lead to a shopping addiction. It saps the compulsive shopper's energy and deepens the distance between true self and protective mask.

Claudia's obsessive need to buy image stemmed from her early childhood experiences. She was born in 1950, the first of three children. Her father had pulled himself up from a poverty-stricken youth, and he was able to settle his family into a small black enclave in a suburban New Jersey town. Yet because of his deprived background, he never felt fully secure in his middle-class existence. He constantly counted pennies and begrudged all the things Claudia's doting mother bought for her.

"I remember once when I was about eight, Mama took us into New York to shop for Easter dresses. We went to B. Altman's and I picked out a beautiful pink taffeta dress," recalled Claudia. "Mama made us promise to tell our father we had shopped at Korvette's, because he thought Altman's was too expensive. But he found the sales slip and made Mama return our dresses. As punishment we had to wear old things on Easter. We had a little Easter parade in our town, and I remember I refused to go that year because I was so ashamed."

The generosity of her mother and the withholding nature of her father sent young Claudia a mixed message. When there is a disparity between parents' views, the child internalizes an inner world of chaos and confusion. Within Claudia, this confusion manifested itself as self-doubt. For two decades she would grapple with the questions: Who am I? Am I a deserving person? Do I deserve to be loved for who I am? Do I deserve to have control over my life—over my spending habits?

Claudia developed an early awareness of image and class disparities that blossomed into an obsession. "All the wealthy families in our town belonged to the same country club, so their children naturally formed their own clique at school. How I would study them—what they were wearing, how they wore their hair, even the glossy notebooks they carried!" said Claudia. "I tried to imitate them, but of course I never made it into their group. I was sure it was because I never looked good enough for them, because my father wouldn't let me shop in fancy stores."

Claudia was very conscious about class structure and somewhat confused about where she fit in. In order to leave her roots behind and identify with "the beautiful people," Claudia carefully avoided relationships with men of her own class. She dated only wealthy men who could give her the things her father never would and who would provide entree into an upper-class world. Her beauty attracted a series of long-term lovers, most of them married and older. She was always the mistress, feeling undeserving of marriage. As the mistress, she could constantly protect her image, never revealing to herself or her lover the imperfections that are part of being human.

To compensate for not being first in these men's lives, Claudia unconsciously manipulated them into buying her things. Jewelry from Cartier's helped balance the inequity in her relationships. Just as these men had to earn her love with gifts, she felt she had to earn their love by always looking and acting perfect. Her stunning image assured their attraction, attention and love.

She shunned anything flashy. Everything she bought had to be ladylike and elegant, in flawless good taste. This tastefulness also represented an effort to buy her way out of the middle-class status that reminded her of her unhappy youth.

Not only did she purchase couture clothes, she also filled her apartment with expensive objects: antique furniture, Persian rugs, Steuben paperweights and signed fine art prints. She had three sets of Wedgewood china service for 24, sterling-silver utensils, Waterford crystal and Baccarat stemware.

Loans and gifts from her loved ones were imperative in order to finance her upper-class lifestyle. Claudia, like many compulsive shoppers, felt guilty for both her lack of control in the stores and the ensuing dependence on other people. As her already low self-esteem plummeted, her urge to buy soared. She was caught in a self-destructive cycle of shopping to obliterate her pain, then feeling more pain and guilt over her lack of self-control.

Buying Power

Richard pretended he was proofreading the ad copy, but he was actually watching the digital clock on his desk. When it clicked to 5:00, he immediately rose and went to the mirror in the reception area. He combed his hair, wondering if that hundred-dollar haircut really had made his thinning brown hair look thicker. He straightened his silk tie and his Georgio Armani suit jacket. Then he saw his boss standing behind him, ominously waving the ad copy at him.

"I found this on your desk. I thought I asked you to put it on mine when you were finished," she said sharply.

He turned to face her, wishing for the umpteenth time that he was a few inches taller. "I didn't quite finish. I'll do it first thing in the morning."

"The client is coming at 11 a.m. tomorrow. Can't you stay a few more minutes and finish it now?" she asked.

"I'm sorry, but I have an important appointment," he said. "I'm meeting this guy, he's a foreign student and he's going back home to Switzerland tomorrow. He has this fantastic Nikon that he wants to sell, and I know I can get it at a great price."

His boss shook her head. "If you cared about your job as much as your hobby, you might be able to afford a new Nikon."

Richard turned away, unable to face her. He was 32 years old and his boss was only 29, yet she was an account executive, while he was still a mere advertising assistant.

Slipping into his Burberry wool coat was comforting. At least he dressed better than she did. She didn't have luxurious clothes like he did, and she probably didn't have any hobbies, either.

Like many men, Richard considered his shopping compulsion a healthy hobby. Most of his free time was spent buying and selling camera equipment. At night he pored over camera magazines. After work he spent hours in the stores, and on weekends he visited camera expos and conventions.

Yet Richard was not a professional photographer. He rarely used all of the cameras he bought. He appreciated the quality of the equipment he purchased, but his interest lay primarily in the "wheeling and dealing." "There's nothing more exciting than spotting a find and then selling it at a profit," he said.

Richard wasn't solely interested in buying cameras—he was interested in buying power. Getting a good deal or making money on a resale gave him a feeling of power that he lacked in other areas of his life. But he was sabotaging himself. He misdirected most of his energy into the camera game, instead of pursuing genuine sources of power, such as success in his career. He didn't establish intimate relationships. The only excitement he allowed himself to feel was about objects, never people. "I really wouldn't have time for a steady girlfriend, unless she was into cameras too," said Richard.

Being preoccupied with his hobby also allowed him to avoid examining his feelings. It absorbed his consciousness so he could ignore the deeper issues in his life. He was distracted from the deep sense of helplessness and fear engendered by losing his mother and having an ineffectual father.

Clothes as well as cameras were a way for Richard to purchase an illusion of power. When he faced job interviews after college, a wave of panic gripped him. Subconsciously, he feared he would be a failure in the work world, like his father. He had to do something to prove otherwise. He went on a shopping spree, purchasing an $800 Pierre Cardin suit, a $90 designer shirt, and $300 imported shoes. Being clothed in the garb of a successful man made him more confident during his job search. It never occurred to him that "clothes don't make the man."

Over the next decade, he continued to use clothes to mask his insecurity. Dozens of expensive suits served as his armor in the business world. He bought a tuxedo, although he had no occasion to wear it. He purchased beach wear for a vacation he never took. Avant-garde clothes for trendy night spots hung in his closet untouched, because he rarely went to clubs.

Richard bought these clothes so he would feel prepared for any event. His mother's death caused him to feel that the world was a dangerous place where random, unexpected things could occur at any time. Much of his shopping represented an attempt to buy a sense of control in a threatening, unstable universe. He tried to buy the feeling of being a real man, a strong man, a man very different from his father.

Buying for Others

"I love my baby so much, I just can't buy her enough," said Denise, a 31-year-old first-time mother. She wouldn't buy her infant the inexpensive outfits sold in bargain outlets, or even the medium-priced goods available in department stores. She bought only designer clothes in expensive children's boutiques. Many of these outfits were handmade, one-of-a-kind items with elaborate embroidery and applique work, which sold for over $100 each. Denise ignored the fact that these clothes were highly impractical; they stained easily, were hard to clean, and the baby grew out of them in a few months. More importantly, the baby did not know the difference between designer clothes and less-expensive ones.

Denise was obsessed with buying only the best for her child. Her shopping binges included fancy furniture and decorations for the nursery, stuffed animals and elaborate toys that the baby was too young to appreciate. Even the mobile above the crib was handcrafted and costly.

"My husband, Robert, and I fight about my spending. We're supposed to stick to a budget now that I'm not working and less money is coming in," said Denise. "But I apologize, and since the things are for the baby, not me, he forgives me."

Denise tried to stop arguments by making abject apologies, because confrontations reminded her of her parents, who argued constantly. She swore that when she got married, there would be no screaming matches, so she tried to avoid them whenever possible. However, she could not stop the shopping binges that led to acrimony with her husband.

During Denise's decade of working as a nurse, she had spent responsibly and had even built up a small savings. She had not become a compulsive spender until after the birth of her first baby. Having the baby brought to the surface unresolved issues from her own childhood, especially her insecurity because of her parents' turbulent marriage and their lack of affection toward her. She also felt more dependent on her husband financially and emotionally, because her link to the outside world diminished while his remained the same. Not having the self-esteem to accept this temporary situation, she felt very vulnerable. Coupled with the awesome responsibility of being a parent, this vulnerability induced waves of free-floating anxiety. Shopping provided a temporary relief from her anxious cycle of thoughts.

Her binges were also a form of revenge against her husband.

Denise no longer had time for long lunches and lively evenings with her friends, but Robert was still enjoying the stimulation of adult company all day long. This made her jealous. She felt that he was free, while she was trapped in the house. To make matters worse, she seemed to be growing apart from him. She felt that she bored him conversationally, because she had little to talk about except the baby.

Their sex life also went downhill, becoming infrequent and perfunctory. Denise blamed this in part on the 35 extra pounds she had gained during pregnancy and never taken off. Because she and Robert were less physically affectionate than before, Denise felt a return of the isolation she had felt during childhood.

Although she and Robert had discussed sharing responsibility for the infant, and even the possibility of her resuming work and hiring a babysitter, these ideas were abandoned after the birth. "Robert convinced me that staying home for a year would be good for the baby. As for sharing the diapering and all, he's like a lot of modern guys, I guess," she said. "He went to 'parenting' classes and all that, but when it comes right down to it, I do all the work. He can turn over and go back to sleep when the baby starts crying in the middle of the night. I can't."

Her ambivalence about motherhood made Denise feel terribly guilty. She tried to assuage her guilt by shopping for her child. She felt that by buying the best things, she would be the best mother. Shopping also enabled her to escape for a brief time from the routine of caring for her infant, which she experienced at times as tedious and demanding. She also sought escape from the envy and anger that were tainting her relationship with Robert.

Many compulsive shoppers overspend on their families beyond the point of generosity. They may buy inappropriately extravagant gifts for anniversaries, birthdays or Christmas. They may smother members of their family with presents all year round, ignoring both their own budgets and the mixed feelings these gifts arouse in recipients and givers. Gifts may be an attempt to make up for not giving their loved ones what they really need—attention, love and time together. They can also be an attempt to gain the attention, love and respect they feel is lacking in their lives.

Buying Friendship

"I spend a lot of money entertaining, but it isn't just for kicks, it's for networking," said David. He believed it was important for an entrepreneur like himself to cultivate people. The only way he knew how to do that was to "wine and dine" them.

He frequently took people out to fancy restaurants—places to be "seen" that did not necessarily serve the best food, but were well-known. He ordered expensive wines and encouraged everyone to order lobster or other costly dishes. David always picked up the tab with a flourish, making sure everyone noticed his largesse. Every month, he ran up his credit-card bill to the limit.

"I want everyone to know I'm doing well, and what better way to show them than by picking up the check?" argued David. Through his extravagant gestures, he hoped to win the respect that he lacked internally. He also hoped to win friendship, but his behavior attracted users—shallow, grasping people who were only along for the free ride. They tended to drift away as soon as the next "gravy train" arrived, leaving David just as lonely and empty as before. With women as well as men, his contacts remained on a superficial level. He dated only beautiful, model-type women who were appealing on the surface and made good impressions, but with whom he failed to make any intimate emotional connections.

David had no close friends, but he had a wide circle of acquaintances who attended his frequent, lavish parties. He slavishly read periodicals to discover party ideas, then created menus that reflected the magazine ideas, not his. The parties were always catered, but he didn't relax and let the caterers do their job. He kept looking over their shoulders to make sure that everything was perfect. When he threw a dinner party, the silverware was sterling, the napkins and tablecloths were linen, the goblets crystal, the flowers fresh and abundant. The food was the latest nouvelle cuisine, the wine vintage and a lively group of musicians serenaded the guests. He entertained like a millionaire, when in fact, he had very little money in the bank.

"Last July 4th, I rented a boat and took thirty people out on the river to see the fireworks. It felt so good to glide by all those people on the riverbanks who had to strain and struggle to see. Then we cruised by Malcolm Forbes' boat. I really felt like a winner being out there next to him," said David.

One New Year's Eve, David invited two hundred people to a party, pulling out every name in his address book. David was on a high for a month before the party, imagining how impressed everyone would be and how many important friends he'd make. He also gloated over how shocked his parents would be if they knew about the bash.

The party was held in a hall, where glittering people exchanged trivialities and swayed to the live band's music. Thirty-eight types of hors d'oeuvres were served and 30 cases of expensive champagne were consumed. The party was far too crowded and noisy for David to make any meaningful or lasting contacts. If people were impressed with his extravagance, they were too busy gulping champagne to tell him. All David got out of it was a hangover and a $14,000 bill.

Unlike Claudia and David, some compulsive shoppers fixate on one type of purchase. Certain items become imbued with symbolic significance. They serve as placebos for people seeking inner experiences that cannot be bought. Because they reflect deep unfulfilled needs, particular objects exert a tremendous psychic pull. Lured by the false hope of attaining emotional qualities that are sadly lacking in their lives, people continue to buy things they already possess in abundance.

As you read through the following case histories, notice the symbolic meaning of the items these compulsive shoppers buy. Note how they represent what is lacking in their internal lives. This will give you a new way of looking at your own spending patterns and may provide insight as to why you feel drawn to certain purchases.

Buying Nurturance and Reassurance

"It's just so much to handle—a full-time job, plus two little kids. Sometimes I wonder if I can go on," said Jamie. Her relentless perfectionism added to the high level of pressure in her life as a working single mother with a full-time job. It was not enough that she do it all, she had to do it perfectly.

However, because her own mother had not provided a nurturing role model, she was ill-equipped to deal with the difficult circumstances of single parenting. She sought relief from this pressure by shopping for items for her kitchen and bedroom.

Jamie was a multiple shopper—she often bought a number of identical items. Tucked away in her cupboard were multiple items such as three teapots, 24 dish towels, three sets of dishes for 24, four sets of silver, and dozens of goblets untouched by wine or water. These kitchenwares represented the nurturing mother-love she never had. They also served to make Jamie feel that she was a good mother, providing abundant cookware with which to feed her children. She felt guilty about leaving them with a babysitter while she was at work, so she bought these housewares to maintain her connection with home and hearth.

When her husband moved out, she decided to redo her bedroom completely, erasing all traces of their unhappy marriage. She started buying bedroom items obsessively, racking up enormous credit-card debts. Yet no matter how much she bought, her bed was still empty. She went on more shopping binges to stave off her empty reality. Eight pillow shams, six sets of designer sheets, ten sets of flannel sheets and pillowcases, and five bedspreads were all stuffed in her closet.

Her bedroom was a place to escape from the pain and pressure of life. After she put her children to sleep, she usually retreated to her bed, burrowing under a goose-down quilt. "Socializing just adds more pressure, and who needs that? Dates are usually so awkward and disappointing. Having friends over is uncomfortable too, because they're all married and I'm not anymore," said Jamie. "I don't have the energy. I'd rather just relax in bed than deal with all that."

So she retreated to the sanctuary and limitations of her bedroom, surrounded by the fruits of her shopping binges. The abundance of items gave her a momentary illusion of having something of substance. It was comforting for Jamie to lie in bed looking at the antique quilts folded neatly on her quilt rack. For Jamie, as for so many other compulsive shoppers, certain objects represent a temporary and self-deluding attempt to secure love and reassurance.

Buying Popularity

A crowd of over fifty people gathered on a Friday night in front of New York's trendiest new nightclub. They vied to win the attention of the doorman, who handpicked which people were allowed to enter the club. Brad W. stood with his hands in the pockets of his distressed leather jacket, praying he would be chosen. He sported a pair of destroyed denim jeans, motorcycle boots, a Japanese designer shirt with asymmetrical lapels and a spikey short hairdo. This artfully casual look had cost him over $1,200 to assemble, almost three weeks' salary.

The doorman nodded toward Brad and he was allowed to slip through the velvet ropes and pay $15 to enter the club. He felt a moment of triumph, of vindication, for the childhood years of humiliation. He had been the class scapegoat: obese, acne-ridden, easy to mock. He had gone to a local college, where he had done well academically, but remained socially awkward. When he reached his senior year, he panicked at the thought of moving away from home and getting a job.

His parents then sent him to a therapist to help him deal with his problems adjusting to adult life. She helped him overcome his eating problem, and he lost 50 pounds over a period of eight months. He moved to New York City, took an apartment with a roommate and got a job in a graphic design firm. However, he never dealt with the fundamental issues that had created his eating disorder. He replaced his food obsession with a shopping compulsion.

"I remember when I first hit New York, I was so jealous of all those great-looking people with great-looking clothes. I would go to clubs and a lot of times I wouldn't get in. I felt like such a nerd. Then I caught on. I realized that if you look right, you can get in," said Brad. Getting into the clubs represented social acceptance and superiority to those left outside, but the price of admission was much higher than he realized.

Most of his salary was spent on the most outrageous fashions offered by the downtown stores. He wore many of these outfits only once and some not at all. Like many compulsive spenders, his purchases were made in an altered state of consciousness. During these binges, the high of the moment often obscured his rational judgment and taste.

As the discarded outfits piled up, so did his debts. He neglected to make payments on his college loan, and he dropped his health insurance plan. He fell behind in his rent and telephone bills. He paid only the minimum on his credit cards each month, then ran them up to the limit. Juggling money consumed much of his time and energy, leaving him drained emotionally as well as financially. He lied to his parents to solicit loans, saying that his rent was higher and his salary lower than they were. Lying produced enormous guilt, but he felt he had no choice.

On this particular Friday night, the club was crowded with people he didn't know—and never would. The volume of the music precluded the possibility of conversation, except in the co-ed bathrooms where people gathered to trade drugs and gossip. Brad posed against a pillar near the dance floor, adopting the proper expression of feigned boredom. As he watched the couples dance, he felt a wave of anxiety about his attire. It wasn't quite right—he really needed some new things. Instead of trying to make human contact, he planned where he would shop the next day. If he kept shopping, he thought, eventually he'd get just the right outfit. Then he'd have lots of friends, maybe even someone to love. He'd get waved straight into the clubs, and he wouldn't even have to pay admission. He'd finally feel attractive and popular, and he wouldn't be lonely anymore.

Buying Creativity and Adventure

Marsha S., a middle-aged woman, is married to a wealthy workaholic lawyer. She has a daughter who studies modern dance in college and a teen-age son who plays in a punk rock band. Once they reached adolescence, both of her children discouraged her attempts to communicate and showed her a lack of respect. "They don't have time for me anymore," she said. "When they do make it to family dinners, they're not really interested in anything I have to say." Nor did her husband respect her opinion, thinking that she had never done anything in the "real" world. This was primarily because he had always encouraged her dependence and ridiculed her attempts at assertiveness.

After her children rejected her attention, Marsha developed an interest in art. She began to frequent galleries, intrigued by the people in the art milieu. "They seem to lead such adventurous lives. I wish I could be like them, but I guess it's much too late," she said. Marsha started purchasing paintings by young artists, buying her way into acceptance in the exotic art world. Immersing herself in this scene, as opposed to genuinely appreciating art, was a misguided attempt at improving self-esteem.

Initially, her husband scoffed at her art mania, dismissing it as a foolish diversion. Then Marsha began to spend so much money that he was forced to take notice. Not only did she buy art works, but she also spent extravagantly on a new wardrobe of avant-garde clothes so that she would feel at home in the art world. Although they had money, he objected to her spending it on something as "useless" as art and clothing he disliked. They had heated arguments about her purchases. She began diverting money from her household budget to pay for paintings and outfits.

It wasn't simply the visual appeal of the paintings that was so magnetic, it was what they represented—the risks and rewards that she lacked in her safe but unfulfilled life. Marsha, who had never been able to make a statement on her own, was hooked on buying other people's statements.

Buying Sexuality

Some people try to buy love with sex. They try to buy an aura of sexuality by overspending on expensive lingerie, toiletries and boudoir accessories. Kim G., an attractive editorial assistant in her late twenties, was panicked by the news media hype about the man shortage. She was desperate to "hook" a husband before she turned 30. Not valuing her intrinsic self-worth, she thought perhaps sex was the way to get a man. "There are just so few available men out there, a girl has to do everything she possibly can," said Kim.

Prior to receiving a large inheritance, Kim got herself $7,000 in debt trying to purchase sex appeal. She redid her bedroom with romantic lighting and satin sheets. She installed a new bathtub, big enough for two, and bought bottles of costly lotions and perfumes. Her drawers were soon overflowing with lingerie: lace teddies; garter belts, stockings and pantyhose in a slew of colors and patterns; silk panties and slips; designer negligees; Japanese kimonos; merry widow corsets and push-up bras; satin tap pants and camisoles.

"If I think I'm going to go to bed for the first time with a man I've been dating, I'll go out and buy something really sexy. I never buy cheap stuff, because that might make me look cheap. I buy real silk, classy stuff," said Kim. "Then I know he'll be really turned on."

She told herself she was buying the garments to be attractive to men, but it was actually a form of compensation for her deeply felt insecurities. Although she found it painfully difficult to be without sex, she enjoyed it less than many other women. Instead of exposing her true needs and desires to her partners, she often faked orgasms, fearing she'd be rejected otherwise. She was erratic in her ability to climax, but constantly craved being held and stroked. What she truly wanted from sex was to feel loved and to merge with another human being.

The seductive lingerie served several purposes. Kim enjoyed her provocative appearance—it was fun. It was also a means of feeling some control in an area that often inspired frustration and self-denigration. Creating a sex goddess illusion helped her delude herself.

Buying Control

Although she was 24, Marie still lived at home with her parents. She did not do this out of devotion. She lived with her parents in order to save money on rent and all the household items she would have to buy if she were living alone. Her parents were self-sufficient and even suggested that she get her own place. She made enough money to support herself at her job as a dental hygienist, a position that she had held since graduating from high school. It was a routine, tedious job, but it was secure. However, she did not have the confidence to move on to anything more challenging.

Marie did not put the money she saved into a bank account or other investment. She spent every extra penny on exercise clothes, clubs and equipment.

She had eighteen pairs of exercise shoes, from jogging shoes to aerobics shoes to jazz dance slippers. An eight-drawer dresser was filled with nothing but leg-warmers, tights and socks in every hue, texture, pattern and material. Another large bureau was stuffed with leotards: classic ballet-style leotards in six different shades; shiny, shimmery leotards in bright, bold colors; striped v-neck cotton blends; swimsuit-style, polka-dot and abstract-design leotards. Marie never stopped to count them, but there must have been over a hundred.

She purchased two large cardboard storage units to house her vast collection of shorts, dance skirts and jogging pants. Another cardboard-constructed bureau held workout tops, from faddish pre-ripped sweatshirts to dozens of T-shirts and tank tops. She also had fourteen swimsuits for lounging in the health club hot tubs, all kinds of headbands, and even wrist weights to match her different outfits.

For the rare days when she didn't make it to the health clubs, she bought a full set of Nautilus equipment and exercise mats and set up a mini-gym in her parents' basement. She had exercise videotapes and bought several new exercise books each month. By pounding her body into perfection and buying exercise clothes similar to what the workout celebrities wore, she was able to identify with them. She fantasized that she was like the talented, gorgeous movie stars who led exciting, glamorous lives. It provided an escape from the tedium of her own existence.

"I'm famous at the club for never wearing the same outfit twice," Marie said. She belonged to two different health clubs, one near her home, which cost about $800 a year to join, and a very posh one near her office that cost more than $1000. "I have to look good at the clubs, 'cause that's where you meet guys. With all the competition, you've got to do something to make them notice you."

Actually, with her long auburn hair and tall, slender, well-muscled body, Marie had no trouble being noticed by men. She went on many dates, but none of her relationships lasted longer than a few months. After working and exercising, she had little time left over to read, go to movies, meet new people or otherwise cultivate her mind and spirit. She hadn't created for herself a well-rounded life. Therefore, her dates found her one-dimensional.

Time passed and she watched her friends getting married and starting families of their own, while she remained single and lonely. "It seems like all the good guys are snatched up already," she lamented. "Only the users and losers are left."

In her relationships, Marie felt powerless. The men did the calling, made the plans, made the sexual advances, and finally did the breaking up. She thought she was being feminine and appealing by being so unassertive, but she was coming across as a weak woman who would not be a desirable partner.

Giving herself over completely in her relationships, yet having them be unsuccessful, caused Marie to experience a great deal of "free-floating anxiety." This type of anxiety results when people do not confront their fears directly, keeping them repressed but very much alive in their subconscious.

Instead of facing her fears, Marie ran away from them. She jogged on the treadmill in the health club. Sometimes she spent an hour working on the "Stairmaster," a machine that simulated climbing stairs. As she climbed to nowhere, she tried to convince herself that if she had control over her body, she had control over her life. But her myth was slowly disintegrating.

The nature of exercise is expansive and it is renowned for its anxiety-releasing qualities. For people like Marie, however, exercise is an addiction. It is a ritual that helps them feel in control. It is a way to temporarily escape from their anxieties, instead of taking steps to relieve them. They hope that if their "outside" is perfect, it will mask and compensate for the deficiencies and frustration within. •

Every time I use a credit card, I feel like I'm living on the edge. I never know how much credit I've used up, or if I'll go over the top. It's a dangerous game. I hate it, but I love it.—***Jamie***

Chapter 5

Living on the Edge

In general, compulsive shoppers are responsible people with very high standards of how to perform in their private and professional lives. Being perfectionists, their standards compel them to please others as well as themselves and to constantly try to do everything right. Having a strict moral code, they usually do not let themselves find release in alcohol, drugs, promiscuous sex or other common, "bad" outlets. Compulsive shoppers do not live on the fringes of society. They are "good" people who live on the edge.

Although compulsive shoppers generally are traditional in their lifestyles, they crave the thrills and excitement that they do not create in their lives. They become bored as a result of being uncomfortable or out of touch with their inner selves. They have no sense of the excitement that can be brought to most aspects of life. They deny themselves stimulating experiences and relationships, sticking to a routine, limited existence. Only in the realm of shopping do they let go of control, stop trying to be "good" and experience perilous excitement.

The following narratives are dramatic stories of living on the edge—and falling off it. They underscore the danger that is inherent in compulsive shopping. When you read in later chapters of the progress and recovery made by these individuals, you will fully appreciate how far they have risen from the depths to which they had fallen.

Credit Card Gambler: Jamie's Story

"I had twelve credit cards, all the big department stores plus *all* the major cards. They kept sending me offers for new ones and I always accepted. Having all the cards made me feel like I had a lot to spend, even though I really didn't.

"I never carefully checked my monthly statements. I especially tried to avoid noticing the full amount that I owed. I didn't want to know. I just paid the minimum and stuck them in a drawer. I would never add new receipts to the balances. So when I went shopping, I never knew if I had enough credit left to make my purchases.

"I would get so nervous and excited when it was my turn at the cash register, and the salesperson checked my card. It was like standing at a roulette table. Would my number come up a winner? Or would I have to face the humiliation of being told I had exceeded the limit? Not knowing whether I would win or lose the credit card gamble gave me this tremor of excitement inside. It was such a different feeling.

"Sometimes when I paid the minimum on my cards, I couldn't help seeing what I owed. I remember when my Sears card had only $25 left on the limit. I went to Sears anyway because I needed a new saucepan—the ones I had were kind of scorched and old. Well, they had this whole set of heavy stainless steel pots and pans on sale for only $89. I started thinking how nice it would be to get the whole set, so they'd all match, instead of buying just one. I took the set up to the register and I gave the girl my card. My heart was pounding. For some reason, it went through. When I heard the register ringing open, I felt like I had won the jackpot!

"I kept ringing up and ringing up those credit-card bills. Somehow, because I was paying with plastic instead of cash, it didn't seem like I was really spending money.

"One time I was just coming out of a depression. I felt guilty because I had been kind of grouchy with the kids for a couple of weeks, hadn't had much energy for playing with them or anything. So I decided to buy them some new clothes to make up for it. I went to the mall where this new children's boutique had opened. They had a line by a company called 'Shy Girls' of hand-appliqued sweatshirt outfits. They were expensive but adorable, and I bought my little girl six different styles. Then I figured I had to get my son just as much, so he wouldn't get jealous. I bought him six different designer outfits. I charged them all. My daughter looked like a doll, and she was delighted with the clothes. I felt proud looking at my son, although he was too young to know how cute he looked. It also made me feel better about myself when my friends could see my kids looking so special. But I still felt guilty about spending so much.

"I got to the point where I had rung up the cards so high that I had trouble paying even the minimums. I asked my husband for money. He really ripped into me! He said I was getting a fair amount of child support, and if I couldn't control my spending, I should go see a shrink. I guess he was right, but at the time it just depressed me. I had a feeling when I asked that he wouldn't give me a cent more than he had to, especially now that he was remarried.

"Then I asked my father for a little to tide me over, and he gave me a few hundred. My mother, who's in charge of balancing their checkbook, got wind of it and kicked up a big fuss. She complained that he gave me money while she had to make do with old furniture and worn carpeting, and I had so many new things.

"You'd think I would stop spending, right? But I didn't. Instead, I started being late with the insurance bills, the phone bills—once they shut my phone off because I didn't pay. Once I neglected to pay the utilities for so long that they cut off my power. I was so overwhelmed by all the bills, I didn't realize I hadn't paid that one until the house went dark. Still, I kept racking up those credit-card bills. It got to the point where I couldn't meet my mortgage payments. I had to put the house up for sale. I decided to live with my parents for a while, until I could somehow get back on my feet. I knew it wasn't going to be easy, but what choice did I have?

"It was a devastating decision, both for me and for the kids. My little girl had already started school. Because my parents live in another town, she had to be yanked out and start with a new bunch of kids, which is always tough. My son was taken out of nursery school and had to leave his little buddies on the block. Oh, how they cried and cried! And me too! I felt so sad for all of us as I hugged my next-door neighbor good-bye. I felt so guilty. One of the reasons I had bought all that stuff was to try to make the kids happy, and now I was making them absolutely miserable. I felt bad for myself as well. I felt like such a failure moving back home. I wasn't looking forward to living with my mother again. I knew I was in for a lot of criticism, and I didn't need it because I hated myself enough.

"Both my parents came to help me pack up. It was quite a shock for them to see how much I had accumulated. It was a surprise for me too. I had absolutely no idea how much I had! Things I didn't need, things I had never even used. I had multiples of the exact same items—that was the most humiliating! When my kids and I walked into my parents' house, and I looked at my mother's face, I felt like a child again. At that point I couldn't deny that I needed help."

Jamie never realized the full extent of the danger of credit cards, if misused. Although she knew intellectually that they represented money, at the moment she was making purchases she felt she wasn't really paying for her shopping binges. This is a common fallacy. For the compulsive shopper, credit cards can destroy common sense and good judgment and create the illusion that purchases are free. Credit cards can invoke an automatic response that promotes spending. There is a false illusion of availability of money when compulsive shoppers do not have to reach into their wallet for money or a check. When payment is in the future, it often doesn't feel real in the present.

It was only when Jamie's parents helped her pack up her possessions that she realized the extent of her shopping addiction. Her mother insisted that Jamie have a garage sale, because there was not enough room in their house to store all her things. This garage sale was an unforgettable experience of public humiliation. Although no one commented, she felt certain her neighbors knew she was an out-of-control spender when they saw the contents of the sale. However, the episode had a positive effect. It forced Jamie to come to terms with her addiction and seek help.

The Juggler: Richard's Story

• • • • • • • • • •

"The ad agency where I work is right near a fantastic camera store. At lunchtime, I would wander through the store, looking for special sales, maybe picking up a new lens or a filter. I went in there so often I got to know one of the salesmen, a guy named Roger. If I saw a used camera that was a good buy, or something new, Roger would show it to me and explain how the focus worked, the special features and all that. I guess he liked to talk about cameras as much as I did, and we got into some pretty long raps. Sometimes I was late getting back to work, and my boss would get on my case. She didn't like me because I wasn't a workaholic like her.

"I guess she didn't give me rave reviews to the higher-ups, because when raise time rolled around I never got much. Cost-of-living raises were all I ever got, while I'm sure other people got big raises and also bonuses. My lousy raises were hardly enough to keep up with my rent increases, let alone my camera collection. I didn't want to cut down on buying equipment, so I kept spending—not only on cameras but also on clothes. Other people at the agency might make more money, but I looked better, and my camera equipment was really impressive.

"Things were getting really tight, so I applied for a bank loan. I lied on the application, said I was using it for a computer course so I could further my career. They gave me a loan for $3000. It went quick.

"I usually used credit cards for clothes. I'd whip one out, and it hardly seemed like I was paying at all—until the end of the month. Then I would pay the bare minimum. One of my major credit cards got canceled because I couldn't pay it off on time. Later on, they cut off future credit on all my cards. I was left with nothing but a bunch of plastic to remind me of how much I owed. And that 18 percent interest was a killer!

"I was also having trouble paying the rent on time, so I advertised for a roommate. The people who came in response to the ad couldn't believe how much camera gear I had around. They all thought I was some hotshot photographer. The problem with the roommate situation was that my place is only a small one-bedroom, and nobody wanted to sleep in the living room, so I ended up doing it. I gave my roommate the bedroom. I slept in the living room, surrounded by my equipment. I had to hang my clothes on garment racks because there was no closet space out there. I still kept buying new clothes, even though I couldn't afford my own closet anymore.

"I really didn't look forward to coming home, especially since I had to face a pile of mail about my debts. Not only the credit cards, but also a student loan and unpaid traffic tickets from ages ago. Letters from collection agencies, letters threatening to garnishee my salary—I didn't know what they could really do and what was just scare tactics, but it all made me miserable. I got phone calls day and night from collection agencies! It drove me up the wall. I felt like I wasn't safe in my own apartment. I certainly wasn't comfortable there, with my roommate stepping over me every time he went to the bathroom. This wasn't the way I pictured myself living, at my age.

"I tried to stay away from the apartment as much as possible. I went to camera shows all over the place. I went shopping until the stores closed. I tried to tell myself I would just browse, but once I was in the stores, I couldn't resist buying. So I was spending more than I was saving by having the roommate.

"Juggling money was like a second job. I'd stay up late at night trying to figure out ways to juggle bills. Sometimes I'd pay a little on one debt just to keep them from doing something drastic, but that would only make me late with another bill. I did some pretty outrageous things. Once when I got a late notice from the gas company, I called up and pretended I had never received the bill. I told the bank I had mailed in a check payment on my loan, and they must have made a computer error and not recorded it. When one collection agency said they were going to take legal action against me, I told them I had just sent a payment, and it must have gotten lost in the mail. None of these stupid scams worked, of course, but they gave me a sense of being off the hook—if only for a day or a week. Still, let's face it, there was no way around my bills. I wasn't sleeping well, and I made a lot of mistakes at work. I felt like my life was falling apart.

"In the middle of this financial crunch, I spotted a Hasselblad camera on sale at my favorite store. A Hasselblad is the Rolls Royce of cameras, and they last forever. The price tag was $1500, but I bargained Roger down to $1350. I was sure I could resell it for much more. I had only about $1000 in my checking account and nothing in savings, but I just had to have it! I wrote a check out for the camera and carried it home, practically shaking with excitement. However, that night I couldn't sleep. I was panicked thinking about how the check was going to bounce.

"I stayed away from the store, but Roger knew where I worked and he called me up. When he told me the check had bounced, I pretended to be completely surprised. 'Oh how stupid of me,' I said, 'I forgot to transfer funds from my savings to my checking account. I'm really sorry for the oversight. Could you redeposit the check and I'll put money in the account right away.'

"I tried to borrow money from some friends and from my roommate, who'd given me money before. However, by now they were fed up and decided not to bail me out this time. I tried to sell one of my cameras, but I couldn't do it in time.

"I felt nauseous every time the phone rang, thinking it might be Roger. He didn't call; instead, he showed up at the entrance of my office building. Seeing him face to face was the worst. He had been sort of a friend, and now he thought I was less than dirt. It was so embarrassing to have him look at me that way—with a mixture of pity and disgust. He told me I had 30 days to pay, and after that the store would take action. He looked like he was going to punch me out any second. On the way home from that confrontation, I literally got sick right on the sidewalk.

"I work in a huge agency, and we have a department called 'Human Resources.' It takes care of benefits, paychecks, hiring, sick leave and all that. I went down there and asked if I could see someone about getting a salary advance. They sent me to this very nice woman, a real motherly type, Mrs. Russo. She asked me why I needed the advance. I started saying that someone was sick in my family, and I had to help them out. I was so nervous she saw right through me. She said, 'If I'm going to help you, you have to tell me the truth.'

"I guess I really needed to talk to someone, because I let it all gush out. I told Mrs. Russo all about spending too much, about my debts and juggling money. When I got to the part about Roger, I actually started to cry. I never cried in front of anybody before. When I was finished, she said she could grant me a salary advance, but she would also like to see me get professional help. She said she knew of a support group for people with shopping problems. I took the advance and also took Mrs. Russo's advice."

Although debtor's prisons no longer exist in the United States, many compulsive shoppers like Richard create their own jails. He was trapped and desperate, with nowhere left to go. Recognizing that he was on the edge of losing everything—his job, his apartment, his friends, his possessions—he finally took the first step toward accepting the fact that he was an addicted spender.

The Shopping Artist: Marsha's Story

"I studied art history in college before I dropped out to get married, but I let my interest slide over the years. I was busy raising the children and taking care of Justin. It was a satisfying life for a long time—the kind of life I had been brought up to expect. Then the kids got older and didn't have much time for me. Justin was made a partner at the firm and started working very long hours, so I was left with a lot of free time on my hands.

"A new art gallery opened up in my town. I stopped in often and got to know the owner, a woman named Cleo. Although we're about the same age, she seemed much younger than me. When I compared myself to her I felt uneasy, uncomfortable about myself. She always had striking haircuts and wore unusual clothes and jewelry. She had this exciting career, while all I had was a family that didn't have time for me anymore. Meeting her really started me thinking about what I was missing. I guess I was angry and confused.

"She took me under her wing, so to speak, and we had long

conversations about art. It reminded me of those college days when I'd stay up late with friends, drinking wine and talking about art and poetry and music. It made me realize that I had been stifling that part of myself for decades, playing the role of the perfect housewife.

"Cleo began introducing me to some of the artists she represented—unknown, struggling young people. Some of them were so nice and sincere, I felt almost obligated to buy their work after meeting them. I began writing checks for paintings and sculpture.

"I had an idea that I would use the art works to redecorate the house, but Justin wouldn't have it. He didn't appreciate abstract art at all, and he ridiculed my choices. When I told him how much they cost, he was appalled. He told me to resell them, which I couldn't do because the artists were unknown. After a huge argument, I put the pieces in the basement.

"Cleo frequently went gallery hopping in the city, and I started joining her. She knew many of the gallery people and began introducing me. I was put on mailing lists and began to get invitations to the openings. The openings were always crowded with interesting-looking people, drinking white wine and chattering away. They seemed to have so much to talk about and were fascinating compared to my suburban friends. I wanted very much to be part of their world.

"I had always dressed well, but conservatively. I decided that in order to fit in at the galleries and the openings, I would have to change my look. I started shopping in the SoHo boutiques, instead of the suburban stores. I bought avant-garde Japanese and English designer clothes, mostly in black. I must admit I felt strange in them when I first tried them on, but I wanted to belong in the art world.

"When I started appearing in new outfits, Justin would shake his head. He made comments like, 'What do you call that?' or 'Isn't that kind of dress only for kids?' That hurt. He wouldn't let me wear my new clothes when I went out with him and his clients or colleagues. He said he was embarrassed to be seen with me 'looking like a freak.' Several times, I actually had to change my entire outfit right before we went out.

"Since we went out often, I still needed some clothes that he would let me wear, so I started shopping for two wardrobes, one arty and one conservative. Sometimes I would buy three or four outfits a day. I was spending a lot, and Justin started to complain about it. I tried to pin the blame on him, saying he was forcing me to buy clothes I didn't want. Of course he saw the holes in that argument. It's impossible to win an argument with a good lawyer.

"I kept spending and spending on my new look. I bought unusual hats, hand-painted scarves, one-of-a-kind belts, wild hosiery and shoes. I always noticed the women at openings wearing interesting jewelry, so I purchased large handmade silver earrings, coral and ivory necklaces, antique pins and big jangling bracelets. I tried to make myself a walking piece of art. Justin made fun of me and so did my kids. Even my son, with his punk-rock haircut, thought I looked 'weird.' My daughter—on one of the rare occasions when she came home from college—thought my clothes were 'inappropriate.' I guess they preferred the boring old Mom they were used to.

"While I was shopping like mad for clothes, I was still buying art. When one of those good-looking, earnest young artists would show me around his studio, how could I refuse? I started storing pieces at Cleo's gallery so Justin wouldn't see them. I wouldn't list the checks I wrote in our checkbook, because we had a joint account. However, when the bank sent the checks back the next month, he would see them. I guess it was ridiculous to try to stall the inevitable, but I wasn't really thinking straight. I was feeling elated a lot of the time, but anxious also—many new feelings.

"Justin and I had some dreadful fights. Afterward he wouldn't talk for days. There was a lot of silence in the house. This drove me out more, because I needed conversation and companionship. Whenever I left the house, though, it seemed I ended up spending more money.

"One day I saw a sign in a gallery saying they needed part-time help. It seemed like a perfect solution! I could be a part of the art scene and also make my own money so Justin wouldn't be able to complain about my spending. Of course, I wouldn't be making much—only $6 an hour for about 20 hours a week—but it was something. I took the job, which was basically a receptionist position. I answered the phone, showed people around the gallery, worked on mailings and did a little typing.

"The gallery was open until 7 p.m.. By the time I took the train back home, it was at least 8 p.m. Justin always liked to eat about 7:30, and now it was impossible for me to have dinner on the table by then. I was willing to start cooking at eight, but he was inflexible. This made me very angry, because there had been plenty of nights when he worked late and couldn't make dinner. We had a big argument, and he said, 'You're not doing your job!' I said my job was at the gallery, but he insisted it was at home. He ridiculed the amount of money I was making and said I was a dilettante. It really hurt to hear that, maybe because there was some truth in it.

"It seemed that Justin wanted our lives to remain the same, fixed in a pattern that was satisfying to him but not to me. He seemed so rigid and old-fashioned compared to the people in my new world. The dinner issue exemplified his refusal to make concessions for my happiness. I was determined not to back down.

"We had many bitter fights. One day Justin looked at me and said, 'What happened to the girl I married? Why can't you be like you used to be?' He said I was becoming a stranger, a stranger he didn't even want to know. I think Justin was so threatened by the new me that it was impossible for him to be open to the changes in my life. Our marriage was filled with resentment on both sides, and I felt stuck. I loved him, but I wanted him to be flexible enough to enter my new world and enjoy it with me. I really didn't know what to do.

"One day I got so upset thinking about Justin that I dashed out of the gallery and bought $3000 worth of clothes. This was one of my worst binges for many reasons. Justin saw the bill and became very angry, but very quiet. The next morning he said, 'We have to talk.' Then he said, 'Marsha, I'm thinking of leaving you. I need to get away. You don't seem to be trying to make our marriage work anymore. I always thought of you as my best friend, and now I don't even know who you are.' We argued for hours, but I never felt heard and there were no compromises. A week later, Justin moved into a hotel nearby."

Marsha was perfectly valid in her desire for a life of her own. However, it was not valid for her to attempt to buy this new life with money her husband earned. She wanted to have it both ways, to appear to be an independent woman but still depend on her husband's income. Justin, on the other hand, was too threatened by Marsha's changes to communicate with her and try to understand her needs and desires at this stage of her life.

The Beleaguered Borrower: Claudia's Story

"Money issues broke up my marriage. I was married to a fellow student during my senior year of college. He was very idealistic and wanted to do social work with inner-city families. After graduation, I found a position with a good corporation in their communications department, and he went to work for a non-profit agency. My job paid more than twice what his did. This began to bother me. I wanted to upgrade our lifestyle, to move into a nicer apartment and buy better furniture. He couldn't afford to keep up with the changes I wanted to make. He didn't want to get a second, part-time job, and he wouldn't consider switching to a more lucrative field. I realized our values were different. Rather than hurt each other more, we decided to separate.

"After my divorce, I found myself dating only highly successful men. I appreciated the way these sophisticated and often older men treated me. They were gentlemen in the true sense of the word. I felt I had to maintain the proper image in order to feel like the lady I wanted to be. I began spending a great deal of money on clothes. Shopping began to fill up much of my spare time.

"I bought elegant designer clothes, suits, separates and dresses. I reveled in the rich fabrics, the tailoring, the little details like three-inch cuffs and hand-finished hems. I purchased imported hosiery and Italian shoes and handbags to match every outfit. I bought cashmere wool coats, kid gloves and hats to complete the look. Everywhere I went, people began to notice me and treat me with more respect.

"My first serious affair after my marriage was with a middle-aged investment banker, Charles. He introduced me to Cartier's, where he bought me a birthday present: a pair of diamond earrings. How I loved the feeling of wearing real gems! I returned there on my own and bought a jeweled Piaget watch. It was wonderful seeing my co-workers' reactions. But the purchase drained my bank account. When the rent was due, I was short.

"I told Charles that my paycheck was late because of a mix-up in the payroll department and asked to borrow some money.

Afterward, he didn't ask to be paid back, and I didn't offer. I couldn't, because I was still spending every penny that I earned—and then some.

"This happened again, several times. I would make a feeble excuse, and he would lend me a few hundred dollars without comment. I felt a little thrill of excitement when I was in trouble, and he gave me more money than I asked for. I felt well taken care of. There was a part of me that felt uncomfortable about my financial circumstances, but I was not to address that issue for a long time.

"Charles was a wonderful companion, but he was the type of man whose work consumed him. As generous as he was, there was no room in his life for a wife, which became clear to me after a few years. After many separations we ended the relationship.

"Dean, the next man I was involved with, was suave, older, in his fifties. He had a family business that he looked in on now and then, but basically he was independently wealthy. I felt an enormous amount of pressure to keep up appearances with his social group and to please him. I felt I had to achieve a look that was at least as good, if not better, than the women in his circle. It was an expensive proposition. At times I felt somewhat like an imposter. I'd remember my background and wonder where I truly fit in. Most of the time, I buried my doubts. Shopping helped me do that.

"Dean bought me lavish presents—jewelry, furs and objects d'art for my home. I felt I had to upgrade my home in order to be able to entertain his friends and him. I began to buy new furniture, dishes, etc. I often had trouble paying my bills and would ask Dean for help. He must have lent me thousands of dollars over the years. Although he never complained, I felt a mixture of gratitude and resentment. I suppose my resentment started to show in small little ways.

"After we had been together for three years, he announced to me one day that he was getting married to a young woman he had known for only six weeks. I could hardly believe what I was hearing, and he wouldn't offer any explanation. Still, I maintained my dignity and acted like a lady. I didn't get hysterical in front of him, but after he left I couldn't stop crying. I was depressed for about six months after that. As I started to pull out of the depression, I noticed myself spending more and more time in the stores.

"About a year later, I became involved with another older gentlemen, Stephen, a commodities broker. He was married but was separated from his wife when I met him. After our first few months together, he sent me a dozen roses with a ruby and diamond bracelet wrapped around the stems. For our first anniversary he gave me a fur coat, with a pair of ruby and diamond earrings in a box in the pocket. He was very generous.

"Still, no matter how much I had, I always wanted more. Every season there would be new designer collections that I simply had to have. I was making a good salary by now, but it was never quite enough to pay for all my purchases. I used department-store cards and mail-order cards.

"My debts were mounting, so I asked Stephen for a loan. I was rather surprised when he asked when I could pay him back. I told him I would pay him back two months from that day. I was on edge the entire week before I was to pay him back, because I knew I didn't have the money. My heart was pounding when I had to tell him that I couldn't pay him back yet. He said to forget about it, if it was that difficult for me. Had I won something or had I lost something? At that point I wasn't sure.

"I had always been close to my younger sister, Sandra, so the next time I needed a loan I asked her. I felt terrible doing this, because she worked long hours as a real-estate agent and still didn't earn as much as I did. She did, however, give me enough money to pay some of my bills.

"Things between Stephen and me were never quite the same after the incident about the debt. Perhaps I became more self-conscious, but whatever, I felt that I was losing him. So I continued to shop even more, hoping to look so lovely he would stay in love with me. This put me so deeply into debt I had to ask Sandra for another loan.

"This time she became angry with me. I'll never forget what she said. She looked me straight in the eye and shouted, 'I'm not supporting your habit anymore!'—as if I was some kind of dreadful drug addict. The worst part was that she told my parents I had a spending problem and was in debt. My parents had always been proud of my career and the way I looked. Now I had let them down, and they knew the truth. It was unbearable.

"I wouldn't speak to my sister for months because I was so angry. I tried to avoid my parents as much as possible because I was so ashamed. I felt dreadfully alone—estranged from my family and also from Stephen. This estrangement forced me to stop and take a long look at where I was. I was not in an attractive place. I was $35,000 in debt.

"My sister made the first move toward a reconciliation. We met for lunch and had a long talk. She said there must be some type of therapy to help me with my spending problem. I said I would look into it, and I did."

Claudia was creating a no-win situation with the men in her life by assuming that love could be bought with glamorous items.

Perhaps these men would have loved Claudia more if she "let her hair down," but she did not give them the chance. Her insecurity made it imperative for her to keep up appearances at all times, never allowing her humanity and vulnerability to emerge. She diminished herself and her relationships by overemphasizing appearance, while neglecting to express many of her intimate feelings.

Many people, particularly women, are trapped by the notion that they need to look wonderful at all times in order to find and keep desirable partners. This myth is perpetuated by our culture through movies, advertisements, television and more subtle means. In reality, most people are more concerned with their mates' inner qualities than their outer appearance alone. Being kind, accepting and supportive is more important to a relationship than anything money can buy. Projecting self-esteem is more attractive than a designer label.

The Million-Dollar Fix: Kim's Story

"I felt terribly guilty when my mother died because I hadn't visited her in about two months. I meant to go, but I procrastinated because it was never very pleasant. She endlessly talked about why I wasn't married yet. I felt bad enough about still being single without her harping on it. Yet when she died suddenly of a heart attack, I realized that even though we didn't get along very well, she meant so much to me. Once she was gone, I felt all alone in the world. My father had died when I was very young, and I had no brothers or sisters, no husband, no children—nobody I felt I could count on.

"I went up to Boston and stayed in the house. Our family

attorney helped me arrange the funeral. Afterward, it was time to read the will. I was absolutely amazed to find out how much my mother was worth! I knew she was well-off, but I had no idea—the whole estate was worth over a million dollars.

"It was such a surprise because my mother had never acted particularly wealthy. I was stunned by the inheritance. I had always wanted to be rich. I guess everyone does, to some extent, but I had always daydreamed about it a lot. I would look at the beautiful clothes in fashion magazines and fantasize about owning them. I imagined that the women who could afford those outfits had lots of wonderful men to choose from. Now it was my turn. I could make my fantasies come true!

"I had endless meetings with attorneys, bankers and accountants. I told them I wanted to sell the house and the stocks in order to have the cash at my disposal. Of course, they advised against selling and showed me all kinds of figures and investment information. I ignored all of it. I knew I wanted to leave Boston and leave my sadness and guilty feelings behind. I knew I wanted to be rich. I wanted to know I had a million dollars in the bank that I could spend any way I chose. So eventually they had to cooperate with me and put everything up for sale.

"After I received the money from my mother's estate, I quit my job. I had always wanted to have a publishing career, but now it didn't seem to matter. I felt like a different person, and I was going to live in a different world.

"The first thing I needed for my new life was a new wardrobe. I went shopping every day for two weeks, stopping only for lunch. It was the beginning of summer, so I started with bathing suits. I actually bought twenty-one of them. I had always prided myself on having a good figure, and I wanted to show it off, so I bought gold and silver lame bikinis, animal-print maillots, athletic one-pieces and jungle-print bikinis with matching sarongs. I bought oversized silk blouses and chiffon skirts to throw over the suits. I got dozens of sexy sundresses, linen and silk shorts, rompers, cropped tops and lightweight blazers. While I was in the department stores, I couldn't resist going to my favorite section—lingerie. I bought satin designer peignoirs and negligees, an elegant crimson robe, maribou bedroom mules in pink, beige and black, and heaps of pure silk panties. Then I went to the shoe departments where I bought high-heeled alligator sandals in red, ivory and black, silver ankle-strapped sandals, leather thongs—all imported and all expensive.

"When I was done with this two-week shopping binge, I saw a travel agent. She showed me brochures of pleasure spots all over the world. It was so exciting, I could hardly believe it was happening to me! I had seen these places on television, and now that world could be mine. I decided to start off with a summer in the French Riviera. I flew to Nice. I went to St. Tropez, Cannes and smaller towns along the coast. I stayed in luxurious hotels, ate in four-star restaurants and drank vintage wines.

"I met men from all over the world. Some of them were so handsome and charming, they made me feel very special. But none of them were husband material. I suspected that most of the men were married already, although they were pretty smooth at the art of deception. I was also prey to gigolos—gorgeous young men with no visible means of support who latch on to rich women. It was depressing to realize that I was being used not only for sex, but for money as well. After a couple of months I was tired of the sun and the 'beautiful people' and bored with doing nothing but lounging around. So I decided to go to Paris. I had always had romantic ideas about Paris and hoped I might meet the right man there.

"I booked myself into a fancy hotel in the Rive Gauche section. The women there were so elegant—such style and flair. I felt I had to exude that Parisian chic if I was going to compete for men in this city, where looks seemed to count for so much. First, I went to a full-service beauty salon where I had a facial, manicure, pedicure, leg waxing, hair cut and tint—the works.

"Then I decided to do something I had always dreamed about—visit the couture houses. Yves St. Laurent had always been my favorite designer, so I started there. They seated me in an elegant salon and beautiful models paraded the collection in a private fashion show. I picked out a fuchsia strapless satin cocktail dress, a blue taffeta ball gown with an exquisitely embroidered bodice and a little black silk dinner dress with a sequined jacket. They fit me and fussed over me. I couldn't help thinking, 'If only my old co-workers and friends could see me now.'

"The atmosphere at Yves St. Laurent's was so intoxicating. I became hooked on couture. I went to Chanel and ordered three of their classic suits: one slate grey, one red and one navy. Then I went on to Sonia Rykiel's, where I picked out knit separates, all of hand-loomed wool and wonderfully designed. At Hermes I bought leather bags and belts to match all my new clothes. Looking back, it seems like a dream. Even at the time when I was shopping, it had an unreal, dreamlike quality. I never even stopped to ask the prices of the clothes. You know the old saying, 'If you have to ask you can't afford it?' I wanted to feel like one of the privileged.

"Whenever I would slow down and stop shopping, I had to admit I felt lonely and sad. There was no one to show all these purchases to and share my fun with. There was no one to go to the stores or see the sights with. Of course, I met men, but none of the relationships worked out. Partly it was a language problem—my

French was spotty, so the men couldn't fully appreciate my intelligence. The men I found most attractive were either married or dedicated bachelors. It was ironic; I could buy anything I wanted, except what I wanted most—a man to love and marry me. I wondered if I was doing something wrong. Finally I decided it was time to go home.

"I traveled back to New York on the Concorde. The duty I had to pay on all my purchases was incredibly high. In New York, I stayed first in a posh hotel, then I sublet a very expensive furnished apartment on the Upper East Side. Once I was back, my attorney and my banker kept calling me, suggesting that I make some investments. I put them off totally. I suppose I was quite rude. I guess I never understood exactly how much money I had and didn't have, because I thought it would last forever. I remember one phone conversation with the attorney when I hung up on him because he started to reprimand me for being irresponsible. Immediately afterward, to show him who was in charge, I went to Maximilian's and bought a full-length mink coat.

"I started seeing some of my old friends and going out with them to nightclubs, restaurants and shows. I would pick up the tab for everyone because they couldn't keep up with me otherwise. I could spend $2000 in a single evening on limos, dinner and drinks.

"My relationships with men were rockier than ever, and I was feeling restless again. Also, Christmas was approaching. I never felt particularly good during the holiday season, so I booked a flight to the Caribbean. Before I left, I devoured the resort clothing collections.

"I toured the Caribbean for three months, cruising to different islands every few weeks. I stayed in the best suites, surrounded by people, but I felt lonely—especially when I would see couples on their honeymoon trips. I'd console myself by going shopping for perfumes, jewelry and more clothes.

"My life continued in this manner for another year. I would stay in New York for a few months, then get restless and take another trip. I went to California, Hawaii, and Europe again, Rome and London this time. It sounds heavenly, right? But the funny part—the pathetic part actually—is that I wasn't fulfilled. Life is always empty if you have no one special to share it with.

"About a year and a half after I received my inheritance, I decided to go to a health spa in New Mexico. All that rich living had put some weight on me, and I couldn't fit into a lot of my clothes. I went to the bank to withdraw $3000 in traveler's checks. The teller informed me that I had only $2000 in my combined checking-savings account. I was stunned, certain there had been a mistake. I demanded to see the manager. He informed me that it was true there was only $2000 left. I still couldn't believe it. I made frantic phone calls to my accountant and my lawyer. But there was nothing they could do for me. They had tried to warn me, but I had refused to hear them. Now it was too late. The money was all gone.

"You can imagine how much I despised myself. If I had invested some of the money and played it smart, I might have lived on my inheritance for my entire life. But I blew it! It was unbelievable. I couldn't even find consolation in my furs, my jewelry, my immense wardrobe. I couldn't stand the sight of anything that would remind me of my incredible stupidity. There was nothing, no one to console me. I was alone with myself just when I hated myself most. I wanted to die. I just wanted to die.

"However, some instinct for survival made me go on. I got a new job in publishing and found an apartment to share with another woman. When I moved in, she couldn't believe the size of my wardrobe. In fact, it wouldn't fit into the apartment, and I had to rent a separate storage space. My roommate, Julie, became a good friend. Eventually I told her about my inheritance and how I had spent it in such a short time. This was the first time I had opened up to anyone.

"Julie showed me an article about shopping addicts, and it really hit home. It was consoling to read that other people had the same problem I did. Julie encouraged me to seek help. It took me awhile, but I finally reached out."

It is difficult to conceive of anyone spending a million dollars as quickly as Kim did. The fact is that Kim had no more control over the million dollars than she would have had over a hundred. Full-fledged shopping addicts spend whatever they have—and more. They keep spending until they either confront their problem or reach a financial crisis point.

Most members seek professional help after they have experienced severe financial and emotional distress. They are either in debt and/or their overspending has become so extreme that denial is no longer an alternative. They realize that they are addicted to shopping. However, you don't have to hit rock bottom. By implementing the program in this book, you can catch yourself before you fall. •

Until I took a good look at her closet, I had no idea how out of control she really was.—***Frank***

Chapter 6

When the Compulsive Shopper is Your Mate

This chapter directly addresses the spouses of addicted spenders. Feminine pronouns and nouns are used regarding compulsive shoppers in this section strictly to facilitate the ease of your reading; this is in no way intended as a sexist statement. Although the majority of shopping addicts are women, there are also a large number of men who suffer from this problem.

Is Your Spouse a Compulsive Shopper?

Spouses often fail to recognize their mates' shopping addictions until a crisis arises, and the addicted spender bottoms out financially and/or emotionally. One reason for this delayed recognition is that people often deny seeing something painful about their mates. The other reason is that compulsive shopping is just beginning to be recognized as an addiction, after decades of being dismissed as an inability to budget well or a predisposition toward self-indulgence. There is also a cultural stereotype that women love to shop. Consequently, many men dismiss their wives' compulsive shopping as being "typically female."

The first chapter provides clues as to whether your mate is a compulsive shopper who needs help or simply a recreational shopper who has her spending under control. If you study it, you should be able to determine which category she falls into. Shopping addicts can often hide their symptoms from the world, but they can rarely hide them from an enlightened spouse.

How to Tell Your Mate

Most often, the compulsive shopper will be the first person in the relationship to recognize and discuss her addiction with her mate. Frequently, money issues will bring deeper emotional issues to the surface. Sometimes, however, the addicted spender does not acknowledge her problem, either because of ignorance or denial. If this is the case in your marriage, you may have to approach your wife with the truth about her addiction. The compulsive shopper, even if she has strong denial mechanisms, is actually in a vulnerable state. Therefore, if possible, a kind and loving approach is best.

In most instances, the spouse is the most appropriate person to broach the topic of a shopping addiction. Before you do this, ask yourself if you are committed to this marriage. If the answer is yes, try to be gentle with yourself as well as with your spouse, because you are also in a vulnerable state. It is natural for you to have certain fears: Will she hate me for telling her? Will she be able to hear and acknowledge what I've told her? Will she be willing to help herself? Will she recover? Whatever your feelings—anger, hurt, betrayal, fear, frustration, helplessness—this is the time to try to put them aside temporarily. It is best to be clear about your primary goal: to tell your spouse that she has a shopping addiction in a loving and supportive manner, so that if she is ready to hear this, she will. She might deny what she hears from you at first, but maintaining your loving, positive stance is necessary if she is ever to accept it.

It is vital to approach your mate at an optimal time for both of you. The most effective time will be when you're feeling strong and relaxed. This might be after a nice meal, after lovemaking, or after a pleasant outing or good laugh. You, better than anyone, can discern when the time is right.

The very fact that you are telling your wife encourages honesty and closeness between you. It is a difficult task for you, but marriage partners face many uneasy tasks and problems through the years. It's how you choose to deal with problems that can make your marriage strong or weak.

The more reassuring you are, the more receptive your wife will probably be. Preface your statements with loving and reassuring messages. This will only be effective if what you say is genuine. Although I am offering guidelines, they should be adapted so you can be as sincere as possible.

One way to preface your talk might be to say: "Honey, (or whatever term of endearment you use) there's something that I want to tell you that's been on my mind. It's very upsetting to me because I value our relationship (and family, if applicable), and because I'm concerned about you. It may be difficult to hear this. I know what it feels like because there have been times when I had to hear difficult things from you. Still, I'm glad that you told me those things. I always want you to be honest with me because that makes me learn and grow and makes us closer."

Then tell your wife that you think she has a problem with compulsive spending, and you know there are many people who have overcome this problem. This would be a good time for you to say, "I wouldn't be telling you this if I didn't know how strong you are and if I didn't have faith that you can beat this problem."

"Addiction" is a harsh word to bring up at first and should not be mentioned until a later time. This is not the appropriate time to discuss this book either, because it might provoke a defensive reaction. At this point, you might want to highlight examples in your lives when you have seen her compulsive shopping manifest itself.

If your wife becomes extremely defensive, denies her problem, and/or gets furious with you, stop the discussion for the time being. Her reaction might make you feel frustrated and angry, but remember that you can air these feelings at a more appropriate time. You might say to her at this point: "Please consider what I've said, because I love you (and the children if you have them) so much, and I'm concerned about our relationship."

In a few days or a week, your wife may show signs of being willing to explore her problem further. Some of the signs that may indicate her willingness are the following: she might appear less angry; her mood might be better; her body language might invite closeness. There might be other signs that only you can discern. At this time, try again to give her reassuring messages. This reassurance should be a constant underlying theme if she is to feel safe and supported enough to give up her addiction.

Once you feel she is open to it, you can show her the quiz in the first chapter, or any section you think would be most helpful. You might want to discuss people you read about who have overcome their problems. It is crucial for her to hear from you that there is hope and you have faith in her recovery.

Decisions should now be made as to how she will treat the problem. She may want to decide this herself or discuss it with you. The decision is hers. There are several options open to her: using the self-help recovery program in this book; using the book in conjunction with private therapy; seeking professional help; and/or forming her own support group.

Once your wife is clearly involved in a recovery program, you owe it to yourself, to her and to your relationship to discuss all the ramifications her shopping addiction has had on you and your family. If you're honest about your feelings but still maintain a non-judgmental, supportive stance, your wife may share things about you that she would like you to work on as well. Depending on what ensues from this attitude, the trust and intimacy in your marriage can deepen.

After an appropriate time has passed (and only you can judge your own comfort zone), if your wife continues to deny that she has a serious problem, you may want to seek professional counseling.

After reading this section, you should evaluate whether you can *maintain* a reassuring and positive stance once you talk with your wife about her problem. If not, then perhaps a friend or family member who is close to your wife and whom she trusts would be a better person to broach the subject. However, keep in mind that your marriage has the potential for greater strength if you are the one who tells her.

Taking Stock of Yourself

When your wife becomes involved in recovering from her shopping addiction, she will be delving into her emotional life in new depth. It is important for you to do the same at this time. Gaining clarity about yourself, your wife and your marriage can help you be supportive. The following questions will guide you toward insight. As you answer these questions, keep in mind that whatever your responses and feelings may be, they are valid. Try not to judge your feelings, but simply accept them. Voice them at appropriate times when you won't hurt yourself or your spouse.

1. Do you feel guilty because your spouse is a compulsive shopper?

You may feel guilty because you're going through a bad time in the marriage. Perhaps you are fighting a lot, or your work is draining your time and energy, and you're neglecting her. You may feel that her addiction is your fault because you're making her unhappy. It's not that simple! The seeds of her addiction were planted in her childhood experiences, long before you met. If her upbringing created an addictive tendency, she does not need much to push her over the edge. However, there are consequences to one's actions in an interdependent relationship, so try to be mindful of treating her with the love, respect and honesty that are the components of a healthy marriage.

2. Do you feel responsible for finding solutions in order to help your spouse?

If your wife's compulsive shopping becomes the center of your life and your relationship, you will become hooked into the addictive process yourself. You cannot devote all your time and energy to figuring out and solving her problems. You are not qualified to do the work that is best left to professionals. Also, if you attempt to "cure" her, you will end up trying to control her. Attempting to control her will undermine your relationship and probably result in her shopping as a form of rebellion.

The most effective stance is one of loving detachment. Detachment does not mean coldness or non-compassion. On the contrary, it's only by not being enmeshed in your spouse's problem that you can maintain a position of love and reassurance. Remember who you are and who your spouse is. Know that there's a point of separation between you.

You should be willing to discuss her addiction and recovery process when she wants to, but this should not be your only topic of conversation. Cultivate other aspects of your relationship instead of becoming totally immersed in the addiction. Nurture the positive aspects of your life together instead of dwelling on the negative.

3. *Are you honestly expressing all your feelings toward yourself and your spouse?*

Perhaps you are feeling negative about your own life as well as your marriage. You may be feeling angry, betrayed, scared, frustrated, trapped or confused. If you are, these feelings need to be dealt with—not repressed. If you harbor negative feelings, your wife will discern them, either consciously or unconsciously.

Repressed feelings are often manifested in damaging ways. For example, you might blow up over a minor episode when your real rage is over her spending. Or you might attempt to control her by cutting up her credit cards or managing her checkbook. Intimidating actions such as these will retard, not speed, her recovery. It is better to express what you are really feeling than to manifest it in covert ways.

Perhaps you think that you shouldn't burden your wife with your feelings when she is having such a hard time—that you need to be the strong one in the family. However, coddling her this way implies that you think she is weak at a time when she needs you to believe in her strength. By revealing your emotions to her, you are doing several important things. You are implying that she is strong enough to handle your feelings, even during a critical time. You are creating an environment that encourages her to share her experiences during her recovery. You are also showing your respect for the strength of your marriage and its ability to overcome problems.

All couples experience disenchantments, letdowns and hurts. What makes a marriage good is not that it's problem-free; it's that a couple can work through their problems with caring and honesty. Successful marriages involve appropriate compromises, adjustments and negotiations that can only be reached through open communication. If problems can be handled with care and mutual respect, the love and faith that you both desire have a good chance of enduring.

Dealing With Your Anger

The suggestions mentioned here are straightforward, logical and effective. However, because of the particular financial circumstances involved in your marital situation, applying these principles is no easy task.

There is a significant difference between being the spouse of an addicted spender and being married to a person with any other addictive disorder. You suffer directly from your wife's spending compulsion. Your wallet is affected. Your savings are depleted. If you live in a state with community property laws, you are responsible for debts incurred by your wife if she cannot pay them. This is a unique situation. If your wife suffered from another addictive disorder such as alcoholism, you would undoubtedly be affected. The involvement, however, would not be quite the same.

The impact of supporting a spouse in an alcoholic recovery program, for example, is extremely taxing, but the spouse does not experience the physical withdrawal symptoms that his wife suffers. As the spouse of a recovering addictive spender, you suffer the same financial burdens that she does. This is bound to trigger anger and/or panic in you, in addition to the anger and/or panic you may already be experiencing about the tenuous state of your marriage.

If the spouse of a recovering alcoholic feels that his wife is not improving, he can choose to leave. When he does, he will carry emotional debts. However, he will not necessarily carry the financial debts that you may have to carry if you choose to leave your marriage.

Because of the anger and/or panic from the added burden of financial involvement, the application of the suggested techniques might seem to be an impossible task. That is why it is crucial that you learn certain coping techniques for dealing with these feelings.

It is understandable and natural to be angry about the financial burden imposed by your wife's compulsion. It is also important to acknowledge your anger to yourself and to your wife. However, this does not mean that you have to express rage, which can only lead to further marital complications.

Carol Tavris, author of *Anger: The Misunderstood Emotion,* writes about the importance of dampening down rage—or any emotion that leads to inappropriate or self-destructive aggressive behavior—to tolerable levels. "Dampening" these emotions is crucial, not just for the sake of your marriage, but also for the sake of your self-esteem. According to Carol Tavris, "studies show that many people say that their self-esteem drops when they have let themselves express anger."[1] This is not to suggest that you never assert your needs and express your distress, but that doing so through healthy, loving negotiation is best.

If you are on the verge of losing control of your temper, it is vital to either go into a room where you will be alone or leave your home completely until you have calmed down.

If you are overcome by anger or rage, try to do something physical whenever possible. Take a brisk walk, jog, swim, ride a bike, play tennis or racquetball—something to blow off steam.

One way to curb your angry responses is to focus on what you can change, because anger often results from a feeling of helplessness. If you focus on your wife's commitment to change, you will feel less victimized by her actions.

Speaking to a good friend also can be enormously useful in coping with your anger. Feeling understood and affirmed helps you feel better about yourself. Speaking to someone whom you trust allows you to express yourself freely and provides you with a social network. Support from as many of your friends as possible is crucial at this time. This is not an easy time for you, and you need support.

In the event that you do express rage, try to be forgiving of yourself and concentrate on working to diminish it. If none of these suggestions helps you significantly in curbing your angry outbursts, you should consider seeking professional help, either alone or with your wife.

Eliminating Panic

Panic is the flooding of anxiety due to feelings of utter helplessness. If you experience such panic, there are a variety of techniques you can use. Keep in mind that panic represents irrational fear. While the financial threat you are facing is real, the crippling anxiety is due to exaggerated fears concerning the consequences of financial stress. The first step in coping with the panic is to acquire a realistic view of your situation. One way to do this is to see a financial counselor with your wife. Dealing responsibly and realistically with financial matters is a part of your wife's recovery in which you can be involved. You need to develop a financial game plan, a sense of order during this chaotic time. If your energy is directed toward seeking and working out solutions, there will be no panic. You'll be "taking hold of the reins" and feeling more in control. Stress-reducing techniques are relevant and helpful in dealing with your panicky feelings. Dr. Eric Lasser, a clinical psychologist in Ft. Lee, New Jersey, who specializes in stress reduction, has some helpful advice:

"There are proven and generally reliable approaches [for managing stress]. Stress-reducing methods include exercise, meditation, self-hypnosis, social support, and 'behavioral strategies' (i.e., engaging in pleasurable activities on a regular basis with your wife and/or children, as well as on your own; attempting whenever possible to provide at least one instance of daily praise to all family members; being honest about your feelings in a non-retaliatory way).

"Two important points are worth making here. First, there's no one best approach. What works for one person may not work for another. Second, there is no limit to the ways one can reduce stress. Anything that relieves tension, that helps one relax or get through stressful situations, can be an effective approach. It is very much an individual matter. Therefore, one should experiment with various approaches to learn what is best for him/her."

Panic can be a prime cause of anger. If your panic is alleviated, your anger may diminish. As stated previously, acknowledging the problem of compulsive shopping and your attendant anger and/or panic will be a painful experience for both you and your spouse. However, with understanding and commitment, it is possible to come through the fire and emerge a healthier couple. Crises often force a couple to re-examine themselves and their relationship and make necessary positive changes. Let's look at how three couples made it through their crises and ultimately improved their relationships.

From Rage to Understanding
Anne and Jeff's Story

• • • • • • • • • •

Anne had her own checking account, into which she put half her paycheck. The rest went into her joint account with Jeff. As her shopping binges increased in frequency, she depleted her own account and began writing checks from the joint account. That was when Jeff realized she had a shopping problem.

"I was really mad at her," said Jeff. "After all, I didn't run out and buy everything I wanted, so why should she? What with the kids and the house and everything, we had a lot of expenses. She was being irresponsible. You know, we met during those years when a lot of girls were running around, taking drugs and dropping out of school. One of the reasons I was attracted to Anne was that she seemed responsible and sensible. That's what I wanted in a wife. It really got me mad when she started with this crazy shopping. I never thought she was the type to lose control."

Jeff attempted to control Anne's spending through various means: holding her credit cards; searching her for evidence of a shopping binge whenever she came home; and setting limits on how many checks she could write. These controlling actions only served to fuel Anne's anger toward her husband, which was already a motivating factor in her shopping addiction. She found ways to circumvent his control and her spending continued unabated. This infuriated Jeff, and he would berate her until she burst into tears. Then he would stalk out of the house for hours, drowning his sorrows over beer at the local bar. Days of bitter silence between them would follow.

"I'm not a mean guy and I really hate hurting my wife," said Jeff. "I would start out trying to have a talk with her, just a talk, but then I'd get so boiling mad I'd just explode. It really got me teed off that she was acting so weird and spending all our money besides. I just thank God I stopped short of hitting her, because sometimes I sure felt like it. Once I even punched the wall and made a hole in it because I was so mad. I also developed an ulcer, which I blamed on the aggravation she was giving me."

Anne was motivated by these fights to seek help for her shopping addiction. She joined a therapy group for compulsive shoppers and began examining her issues. She realized that in addition to the group, marital counseling was vital to the survival of her marriage.

"At first when she brought up the marriage counseling bit, my reaction was, 'This is your problem, not mine.' But she explained how my anger and my control were also hurting our marriage. It was the first time we had had a real discussion, instead of a fight," said Jeff. "The bottom line was, I knew we were heading toward divorce city. I'm an old-fashioned guy, and I really wanted to keep my family together. So I agreed to give the counseling a try, even though I was skeptical.

"At first the sessions made me feel very awkward. It didn't seem right to hang out the dirty laundry in front of a total stranger. I always felt that I was lucky to be a healthy, normal American, and it was wrong to bellyache about things. But Anne insisted that we keep going to counseling, so we did. Gradually, it started to help. I learned a lot about myself, about Anne, about our marriage. Once I began to understand things, I found I wasn't so angry at her anymore. Things started to get better between us. And you know what? My ulcer even stopped acting up."

The deep connection between psychological and physical health is well-documented. Anger and other negative emotions are, literally, hazardous to your health and can manifest themselves in many maladies. This is yet another reason why it's important to face your feelings and seek professional help to deal with them, if necessary. Marital counseling, as well as individual therapy for both spouses, is sometimes a necessary part of the recovery process for compulsive shoppers and their spouses.

From Betrayal to Respect: Olivia and Frank's Story

"I'd been brought up on those corny old jokes about how women like to shop and spend money, so I never in a million years thought shopping could be a serious problem," said Frank. "I knew Olivia liked to shop all the time, but I thought that's the way women were. I was just glad I could provide for her. I thought, 'She's a good wife. If she wants to indulge in the stores, what's the harm?'

"Then all of a sudden she comes to me and says she's seen this television program about compulsive shoppers, and she thinks she's one. I started laughing. I thought it was a big joke, but I could tell from her face that she thought it was something serious. I asked her why she thought she was a compulsive shopper, what she meant. She started explaining how she went shopping because she felt lonely and insecure. She said she felt better when she was shopping but afterward she felt worse. I was shocked! I thought Olivia was just fine. I never guessed she had all these things going on inside her head. It's funny how you can live with someone for so long but never really know them."

Frank started taking a closer look at Olivia's bills. One day, when she was out shopping, he went up into their attic and discovered bags full of clothes that still had the price tags on them, clothes from years before that Olivia had never even worn.

"I was really stunned," said Frank. "We have money, sure, but it seemed like such a shame to waste it this way. It looked like she wasn't even using, let along enjoying, half the things she bought. I was absolutely disgusted with her. I never thought about the money all these years, and now I felt like she had taken advantage of me. I felt like a sucker. I felt betrayed. But I also felt like she was so mixed up, I shouldn't say anything to make it worse. So I didn't say much about the way I felt."

Olivia joined a therapy group for shopaholics soon after seeing the television program. She tried to discuss the group with Frank, but he cut her off. He was shaken by the intrusion of this problem into their lives and didn't want to talk about it. He had also closed himself off from her to prevent his anger from exploding. He was emotionally withholding because he was afraid of both his own feelings and Olivia's.

After a month in the group, Olivia had gained enough insight to realize that she needed to encourage Frank to communicate. She began asking him how he felt about the situation, drawing him out. Finally he admitted to her that he felt shocked, betrayed and angry. This made Olivia realize, for the first time, that her compulsive shopping could adversely affect others as well as herself. This realization increased her determination to overcome her addiction.

"I'll never forget when I finally let her know just how I felt about the whole shopping thing," Frank said. "I got mad, I even yelled at her, which I never do. But she didn't break down and start crying and make me feel guilty. She accepted my feelings and said she understood. I started thinking that this little lady was a lot stronger than I gave her credit for."

Frank's respect continued to grow as he saw Olivia working on her spending problem without his assistance. She had always been dependent on him, but now she was facing this difficult situation with independence. He was also pleased that she made new friends in the group. Previously, all her friends had been wives of his friends, and these new people added a fresh dimension to their lives.

"Olivia invited two of the women in the group and their husbands over for dinner one night. It was a big relief meeting them, because they were nice, intelligent people. It got me over some of the shame I still felt about the whole situation," said Frank.

He began to respect Olivia's struggle and enjoy hearing about her recovery process. It intrigued him that she was undergoing this self-discovery and growth on her own. His new respect for her brought them closer and revitalized their marriage.

From Frustration to Communication: Lisa and Kevin's Story

"When I first realized the extent of Lisa's debts, I wanted to help her pay them off. I was amazed that she didn't want me to," said Kevin. By this time, Lisa had already learned from her support group that this was something she had to do on her own, even if Kevin had the money, which he did not.

"I hated the feeling of not being in control of the situation. I always prided myself on having things under control, and suddenly the bottom had dropped out," said Kevin. "I just wanted to put everything back to normal. I wanted things to be the way they used to be. But Lisa wouldn't even let me contribute to paying off her debt. It was very frustrating.

Kevin was facing the frustration that people feel when they can't solve their loved ones' problems. If you are feeling this way, try to realize that your mate is a separate individual who must solve her own problems. Bailing her out will only lower her self-esteem and add to her guilt. It also can enable her to perpetuate her addiction by giving her more access to money at a time when she may not have conquered her compulsion.

"Also, it bothered me that so much of her money, for such a long time, would be going to pay off her debt. It was money that should be going to our mutual bills and savings," Kevin said.

Many spouses of compulsive shoppers face frustrating financial circumstances. Remember, however, that couples often face a monetary crunch at some point in their marriage for one reason or another. Loving partners should not let money issues poison their relationship, if they are working to improve the situation.

For several months, Kevin vented his frustration by criticizing Lisa for minor things. He'd make a rude comment about her new haircut, disagree with her in petty ways in public or put down her cooking. Finally Lisa spoke up and said that she wanted him to tell her what was really bothering him. He let his frustration and anger pour out. It was the first time Lisa had ever seen him cry. They wound up in each other's arms, kissing away the tears. It was the first time in many weeks that they made love. It was also the beginning of deeper communication in their marriage.

Several weeks later, Lisa summoned up the courage to tell him about being molested when she was a child. "I was honored that she could finally confide in me," said Kevin. "Knowing what she had been through made me respect her struggle more.

"Also, seeing the way she stopped spending and started paying off her debt on her own made me respect her so much. Judging by the way she's handling her problems, I feel certain that she could handle anything. We both feel that we're stronger partners now and that we're ready to be parents soon. We're waiting until Lisa feels fully recovered. We also want some time to enjoy our new closeness, but we know it's only a matter of time until we start a family. I know she'll make a great mom."

The Effect on Your Children

The effects of compulsive shopping on children are similar to those caused by any marital problems. When adults are embroiled in their own battles and spending great energy overcoming their problems, they often do not pay enough attention to the needs of their children. The children either can become overprotected, or they can become the protectors. In a marriage where problems are not dealt with maturely and honestly, the children are not presented with a model of healthy intimacy.

If the compulsive shopper is seen as weak and the other parent is perceived as strong, their children will learn to see men's and women's relationships as unequal. The concept of equal partnership will be unknown to them. This will prevent them from coupling in an equal, close and communicative way.

The combination of identifying with the weak parent and not having had their needs met can cause children serious loss of self-esteem, which can affect every area of their lives. The children of addicted shoppers may become overspenders themselves and/or may manifest other compulsive behaviors.

I have only briefly mentioned here a few of the effects that problem marriages and addicted parents can have on children. The myriad problems these children face is worthy of a complete book. Therefore, it is essential for the entire family's sake that you and your wife follow the guidelines in this book to the best of your ability.

Avoiding Co-dependence

As we have seen from the preceding anecdotes, it is important to find the proper balance and to be supportive without becoming overly enmeshed in your spouse's addiction. Otherwise, you might experience a condition that is known as *co-dependency*.

Some spouses and other loved ones of addicted people become involved in an addictive process themselves. They exhibit characteristics such as denial, control, thinking disorders, fear, perfectionism, rigidity and loss of personal morality, which are symptoms of the addictive personality. Their relationships to the addicts help co-dependents perpetuate and justify these qualities within themselves. For example, they may feel that it is their role in life to "solve" their loved ones' problems, and they become very controlling as a result. Co-dependents lack personal boundaries and take on the feelings and pain of others. Their lives revolve around the "other" addicted person in their family.

If you suspect that you are a co-dependent, you may want to read up on the subject. The available literature will help you recognize if this is truly your situation, and if so, what you can do about it.

Alternatives

The co-dependency syndrome points up the importance of creating boundaries and not letting yourself become intertwined with your spouse's addiction. In general, it is best if your wife follows the treatment program in this book, joins a support group, or seeks counseling and undergoes recovery largely on her own.

However, each family is different, and the degree of spousal involvement in the recovery process is flexible. Although it is not suggested for most couples, there are some for whom active involvement of the spouse is the best approach.

If co-dependency does not seem to be a problem for you, you might want to follow some of these suggestions. Some addicted spenders find it helpful to shop with their husbands. This helps them make rational choices during shopping and avoid confusion and compulsion. Other couples determine together such financial issues as whether or not the compulsive shopper will use credit cards or a checkbook. Just as an alcoholic may ask a spouse not to have liquor in the house, your wife may want you to hold the checkbook. You might also plan together how much money she will have access to and when, and at what point in her recovery she will resume handling her own finances.

If you take this type of active role, it must be mutually agreed upon. Ascertain that your wife truly wants your help in this manner and is not just giving in to pressure from you to accept it. Be clear that you do not want to control her to satisfy your own psychological needs and there is no power struggle going on. You must feel certain that you can remain equal partners and she feels in no way patronized or controlled. Then, and only then, can your assistance during her recovery period be valuable. •

Doing relaxation techniques makes me sleep almost the way I did before the baby was born. I wake up rested and able to deal better with everything.
—Denise

Chapter 7

Eight-Week Behavioral Modification Program for Compulsive Shoppers

One of the worries you might have before embarking on the recovery program is the fear that you will never be able to shop again. This is not so! Your problem is more comparable to compulsive eating than alcoholism. Food is not banished from the lives of binge eaters; they learn to eat healthily instead of compulsively. Of course you will shop again, but you will shop responsibly and freely, without the chaos, anxiety, shame and depression that attend the compulsive state.

You will be introduced to a series of exercises and techniques that will enable you to relax more, get in touch with your feelings and take stock of your life. You will become more aware of what you want from life and how to get it, so you no longer have to look for it in the stores. You will learn to deal with your relationships and handle your life in a more positive and productive manner.

The Eight-Week Behavioral Modification Program for Compulsive Shoppers presented in this chapter is adapted from techniques used in the Shopaholics Limited® groups. It is designed to enable you to overcome compulsive spending on your own. The eight-week structure is simply a guideline. Everyone has his or her own rhythm of recovery, so the actual time frame will vary. Feel free to modify the program to suit your own pace.

You may feel ambivalent, resentful or afraid that the program will take your "fun" away. These feelings may cause you to panic and go on a spending binge. The best way to handle regressions is to be kind and gentle with yourself. Instead of putting yourself down, congratulate yourself for your courage. Self-encouragement will speed your recovery, while self-criticism will only undermine it. Realize that setbacks and regressions are an inevitable part of the recovery pattern for many people. Do not use the stumbling blocks as a way of lowering your self-esteem and giving up on the program. Continue the program with faith and optimism. Remember that you are not leaving shopping behind forever, you are only leaving behind the confusion, panic and guilt.

Week One

• • • • • • • • • •

Your goals in the first week are:

1. To become *aware* of your shopping compulsion and *accept* that it is a serious problem.
2. To make a firm *commitment* to the recovery process.
3. To think about ways to establish a *buddy system.*

4. To become aware of the emotional signals your body sends you by utilizing *relaxation techniques.*

Awareness and Acceptance

Some of you may have never gone shopping in a relaxed, recreational manner. As a result, you are unaware of the difference between this experience and frenzied compulsive shopping. It is critical that you cultivate awareness of the difference between these experiences so you can recognize fully when you are in a compulsive shopping state. This awareness is fundamental to recovery, because there may come times when you regress into denial. As your awareness heightens, you will find it more difficult to sustain the denial. Eventually you will give up denial and fully accept the reality of your shopping problem. This will motivate you to stick to the program and increase your determination to free yourself from the shopping addiction.

The relaxation techniques you will learn will help you discover what it feels like to be relaxed. They will heighten awareness of your mental and physical state, which will help you fully perceive when you are anxious and confused. Self-awareness will give you a warning sign at times when you are most susceptible to binging and should steer clear of the stores.

Commitment

In this recovery program you will be asked to do a lot of work, both internally and externally. You'll need to look inside yourself and face your demons, dealing with many issues you may never have dealt with before. You will have to learn to assert yourself and bring new honesty and communication into your relationships. You will need to devote time to relaxation and visualization exercises, affirmations, journals, a daily checklist and organizational tasks.

Like most things worth doing, overcoming addiction is not easy—but millions have done it, and you can too. You need to begin with a commitment to yourself: you are worthy of recovery and of living a life free of addiction. Make an oath to yourself that you will do whatever is necessary to break the bonds of compulsion. Treat this oath with the same respect and importance you would give to a marriage vow or other deep commitment.

If you are truly committed to recovery, this means you are willing to work at it. It does not mean that you are expected to become a superwoman or superman and recover in a week or two without setbacks. It does mean you will make recovery a priority in your life. You will keep pursuing this goal despite setbacks, painful or uncomfortable feelings and other adverse situations that may arise.

The Buddy System

The first week of the program is the time to start thinking about who your buddy system will include. A buddy is a person who is willing to help you along the road to recovery. It is best to have more than one buddy to call on, because it is hard for one person to be accessible all the time.

Choose people whom you know, respect, and feel are trustworthy and non-judgmental. They might be friends, relatives or co-workers with whom you are comfortable. Many people find their buddies in support groups, or other groups to which they belong. If you cannot think of anyone who is suitable, you might consider seeing a private therapist to examine why you have trouble establishing relationships. The therapist can, in a sense, be your first buddy. However, try to be open-minded and think of people who might be willing to help you, even if they are not yet close friends.

When you decide whom you would like to have as a buddy and feel ready to broach the subject, ask to meet the person some place where you feel at ease. You can "test the waters" by saying that you have a problem controlling your spending, and you would like to be able to call on him or her for support while you try to overcome it. You don't have to reveal right away the extent of your shopping or the degree to which it has affected your life. As you learn to trust the person, you can reveal more. In time, your buddy should know when you go on shopping binges, how it feels when you're compulsive and how you feel afterward. Take your time in revealing this information, and do it when you feel ready.

Perhaps the idea of telling anyone anything about your spending frightens you. If this is the case, realize that sharing a problem usually brings you closer to another person. The more truth you reveal to your buddy, the more you will learn that you can be liked and accepted for who you are, with your limitations and problems. Showing vulnerability will strengthen and deepen your relationships. Most people will respect you for being open and honest. They may surprise you by responding with intimate revelations of their own. This, too, can deepen your friendship.

Tell your buddy that you chose him or her because you respect his or her sensitivity, understanding, strength, and kind, helpful nature. Most people will be touched and honored that you think they are capable of helping you. However, there may be some people who, for their own personal reasons, will not be able to be your buddy. Try not to personalize this, as it probably has to do with their limitations rather than their feelings toward you. If someone turns you down, go right ahead and approach the next person on your list. If you think positively and really want a buddy, you will find one.

There is no rigid time schedule for developing your buddy system. However, you should cultivate at least one buddy as soon as you can. Having this support will make the other steps of this program somewhat easier.

When you feel the urge to shop, you can call your buddy to explore your feelings. You can also call him or her after a shopping binge, to discuss how you feel and why you overspent.

Your buddy is also someone with whom you can share activities that help keep you away from the stores. For example, if you're of an intellectual bent, you and your buddy might start a book discussion group or go to a poetry reading. You can practice crafts or other hobbies together. You can introduce each other to friends and relatives and enjoy social gatherings. Participating in sports or exercise with your buddy is a good way to let off steam. Use your imagination and do whatever you think you might enjoy—except shopping!

Using the buddy system will help you learn to honestly express your feelings. It will give you a feeling of being supported and grounded. Most likely, the depth of friendship you develop with your buddy will add a new dimension to your life and can lead to the deepening of other relationships.

Relaxation Techniques

Stress is one of the greatest enemies of mental and physical well-being. Scientific studies have proven that stress can contribute to headaches, backaches, digestive disorders, chronic pain and a host of serious illnesses. Stress and its accompanying anxiety can also make a person seek relief through an addictive behavior such as shopping. How often have you gone shopping because you had a tense situation at home or at work?

Stress is inevitable, but practicing relaxation techniques will help prevent it from taking a toll on your physical and mental health. These techniques are far different from activities we often call "relaxing," such as watching television or talking on the phone with a friend. These methods invoke the *relaxation response,* a state in which physiological changes occur. These changes include relaxed muscles, slower breathing, increased blood flow to the brain, and an increase in the brain's alpha waves, which produces a feeling of calm and well-being.

Beginning the day with a relaxation technique will start you off in a calm and aware state of mind and body. It will increase your sensitivity, which will help you track the feelings that might lead to a shopping binge. It will also make it easier to cope with stressful situations as they arise throughout the day.

I strongly suggest that you practice the relaxation techniques at least twice a day, in the morning and in the evening. Some people do these practices immediately before going to sleep (they're great natural tranquilizers). Others prefer doing them as soon as they get home from work. Choose whatever time is most convenient and beneficial for you. The more often you do them, the greater the benefits.

The first relaxation technique should be done in a dimly lit, quiet room where you can lie down comfortably. You can read the instructions several times until you remember them and are able to say them to yourself. You can also make a tape recording of the instructions, or have a friend or family member with a pleasant voice make the recording, and play that back.

Progressive Relaxation Technique

During this exercise, keep your eyes closed and breathe slowly and deeply, through your nose if possible. Lie down on your back on a soft surface; don't use a pillow. Extend your legs and arms comfortably at your sides. You are going to focus on relaxing every part of your body. Take as long as you need to fully relax each body part.

Relax the top of your head. Relax your forehead. Relax your eyeballs. Relax your nose. Relax your cheeks. Relax your ears. Let your head sink into the floor and relax. Relax your mouth. Relax your jaw, letting it go. Relax your throat down to your chest. Relax your chest. Let your shoulders soften. Let your shoulder blades feel very open and relaxed. Relax your rib cage. Relax the middle of your back. Relax your abdomen. Relax your pelvic area. Relax your lower back, letting it sink into the ground. Relax your buttocks. Feel the relaxation entering the deepest level of your body.

Relax your right arm from shoulder to elbow, elbow to wrist. Relax your entire right hand: thumb, pointer, middle finger, ring finger, pinky. Relax your left arm from shoulder to elbow, elbow to wrist. Relax your entire left hand: thumb, pointer, middle finger, ring finger, pinky. Let your arms and hands go. Relax your right leg from thigh to knee, knee to ankle. Let your heel sink into the ground and relax your right foot. Relax each toe. Relax your left leg from thigh to knee, knee to ankle. Let your heel sink into the ground, and relax your left foot. Relax each toe.

Let your entire body relax and sink into the floor. You don't have to be anywhere or do anything. Just be in the moment and relax. Trust that it is safe to let your body relax. The universe will protect you and provide for you. If negative thoughts enter your mind, let them go and return your focus to your breath. Picture yourself letting go of all negativity as you exhale. As you inhale, visualize peace and relaxation with every breath.

Breathing Relaxation

When people are anxious, they tend to breathe rapidly and shallowly, which exacerbates their anxiety. Conversely, when people are very relaxed, they breathe deeply and slowly. By consciously breathing in this manner, you can help relieve and control anxiety.

Breath is life itself, but because it is an automatic function, most people take it for granted. However, practitioners of yoga have practiced controlled breathing for centuries in order to receive the greatest physical benefits and to cultivate a higher state of consciousness. In recent years, health practitioners in many fields have become aware of the importance of breathing and have introduced breathing exercises to their patients.

The best way to become convinced of the benefits of deep breathing is simply to try it. It will take some getting used to, so don't be discouraged if you don't "get it" at first. Like most new things, it takes time and patience. It is worth persevering, because once you have mastered deep breathing, you will know why it is one of the most powerful relaxation techniques. Another benefit is that it can be practiced anywhere, anytime. For example, instead of becoming agitated because your bus is late, you can practice deep breathing while standing in line. You can do it at your desk at work or in bed to lull yourself to sleep. If you're in a compulsive shopping mode, you can sit down on a bench in the shopping area and do some breathing sequences.

Here's how to practice deep breathing for relaxation.

Inhale and exhale through your nose, not your mouth. If you can't do this, use your mouth, but keep working toward breathing exclusively through your nose. As you inhale, think of filling your abdomen slowly with breath. Put your hands on your abdomen; it should fill up like a balloon. Don't exhale; continue inhaling, and feel your rib cage fill with breath. If you put your hands on your ribs, you should feel them moving apart. Continue to inhale, and fill your chest with breath.

Hold the breath as long as you can comfortably, then exhale slowly through your nose. Inhale at least four seconds, counting to yourself. Hold the breath at least four seconds, then exhale for at least four. This may be difficult at first, but it will soon become easier. Work toward inhaling for a count of seven seconds, holding for seven and exhaling for seven. Do this complete sequence seven times.

Deep breathing bathes all your cells with oxygen and blood nutrients and is very beneficial to your health. It also has tremendous psychological effects, creating a sense of tranquility and inner calm. It helps you put your worries into perspective and experience the moment more fully. Learning to experience the present fully aids recovery, because painful attachments to the past or fears about the future lead to obsessive/compulsive behavior. If you are in the moment, you are free of all that psychological weight.

Use deep breathing as often as you can. When you catch yourself starting to have anxious thoughts, stop them by concentrating on your breath instead. Employ the deep-breathing methods. This technique is always available as instant stress relief. You can breathe anytime, anywhere!

Once you have experienced the benefits of these relaxation techniques, you may be inspired to try others. Many people find yoga to be an invaluable stress-reliever, as well as a way to keep fit. Massage is a delightful way to relax. Long, hot baths can be soothing. Explore different ways to reduce your tension.

Now you might be saying, "But I'm too busy!" However, once you reduce the time you spend shopping, you will have more time at your disposal. Second, no matter how busy you are, stress reduction should be a priority. You deserve to take a break from your busy day to practice relaxation techniques. The busier you are, the more necessary it is to replenish yourself. Maintaining a calm state of mind and a relaxed body will enhance all your other activities.

Week Two

• • • • • • • • • •

Your goals in the second week are:

1. To cultivate a feeling of strength and power by using *creative visualization techniques.*
2. To use *affirmations* as daily reminders and positive reinforcement.

Creative Visualizations

What changes would you like to make in your personal life and in your work? How do you visualize the best of all possible worlds for yourself? Do you want to design that world and make it a reality? Creative visualizations will help you become the architect of your own life!

One of the reasons for compulsive shopping is a feeling of ineffectuality and helplessness. Creative visualizations will teach you to stop feeling like a victim. They will enable you to manifest positive changes in your life. Remember the old saying, "As you sow, so shall you reap?" Putting out positive thoughts helps attract positive experiences and people into your life. Learning to let go of negative fears and replace them with positive expectations will have an enormous impact on your life. Imagining the best possible existence for yourself is the first step toward making it a reality.

Creative visualizations teach you to experience yourself as a strong person and a positive thinker. You will begin to believe that you can "seize the reins" and take the necessary steps to improve your life. Taking an active stance will ease the need for compulsive shopping. Remembering the sensation of power and strength you experience during your visualizations will help you withstand the urge to binge.

One of the reasons creative visualizations are so powerful is that they help you tap into your unconscious and get in touch with your higher self. Your higher self can be thought of as your soul, your intuition, your spiritual center. If this part of you is neglected, you may feel a void within and struggle to fill it up with purchases. When you get in touch with your higher self, you feel fulfilled from within. You also increase your effectiveness in the outside world.

The best time to begin your visualization practice is in the morning, immediately after doing a relaxation exercise. Close your eyes and continue to be aware of your breathing. Then imagine yourself doing something difficult and picture it turning out very well. Here are some examples:

- You tell your spouse that you feel you are being taken for granted. Your spouse listens to you attentively, and then sets up a special, romantic evening for the two of you to enjoy.

- In a positive way, you tell your teen-age daughter that you wish she would listen to you reasonably, instead of getting angry at every suggestion. Your daughter responds lovingly and begins to be more receptive.

- You go back to school to learn a new skill that will enable you to get a more satisfying job. You do very well in school and enjoy learning, and when you graduate you get the job you hope for.

- Although you were afraid to try it before, you go on a skiing trip and find out that you're a natural on the slopes. You can visualize any physical activity that you've always wanted to try.

These specific visualizations may not be appropriate for your life; they are merely meant to illustrate the breadth of possibilities. Create your own visualization according to your personal needs and desires. Choose to do visualizations in areas in which you feel limited.

During the visualizations, bodily changes may occur. If they do, pay attention to them. You might feel a surge of power in your legs, or a warmth around your heart. Keep doing the visualizations until these physical sensations become familiar. Then you can try and summon them up in your mind when you need them. When you've had a rough day and crave shopping, invoke the memory of your sense of power as an ally in lessening your need to spend.

Keep the visualizations fresh in your mind, and have faith in them. If you think about the ideal picture every day, it can change your thoughts, expectations and reactions. Visualizations are not miracles. They don't always come true instantly. However, if your goals and desires are clear and constant, your positive attitude will be helpful in overcoming hurdles.

Visualizations can be "taken on the road." You can do them any time or place to anchor yourself and renew your faith in your own strength. They can be used throughout your lifetime for whatever goals you choose. The more you do creative visualizations, the more you will see their remarkable power. Many of the things you imagine may become an integral part of your being.

Affirmations

Affirmations are positive thoughts that are used consciously to replace negative thoughts. Like visualizations, these positive thoughts can become reality. Affirmations are always stated in the present tense, as if to "affirm" that the desirable effect has already occurred. They may not be actualized yet, but you should repeat them with the faith and optimism that they will be. These daily reminders can be a helpful tool in overcoming the negativity that fosters compulsive shopping.

Here are some sample affirmations:

"When I go shopping, I always remember that the objects are less important than I am."

•

"I shop only when I am calm and in control of my emotions."

•

"I take deep breaths whenever I feel anxious."

•

"I am gentle with myself throughout the day."

•

"I have peace, calm and order in my life."

•

"I am self-confident and have high self-esteem."

•

"I love and accept myself."

"I have satisfying, loving relationships in my life."

•

"I take pride in my accomplishments."

The above are guidelines, but you can make up your own affirmations to suit your specific needs. Remember to make them positive, put them in the present tense and keep them simple.

There are many ways to use affirmations as daily reminders. You can set aside a period to meditate on the phrases. You can repeat them out loud, chant or sing them at any time, even when doing the dishes. You can say them to yourself before going to sleep and after waking up, and especially before shopping.

Writing down affirmations is also powerful. You can write the phrase repeatedly on an attractive piece of paper, then hang it up by your bed. You can tack reminders inside your desk at work, on your mirror, on your dashboard—anywhere. You can keep a list of the most important affirmations with you at all times, and read it for sustenance whenever the need arises.

You may be embarrassed to do this or think it's silly. But would you laugh or scoff at the act of praying sincerely? Think of affirmations as an act of faith in your recovery. Part of your recovery process involves opening yourself to new feelings and experiences. If you're willing to try these techniques, you may be pleasantly surprised. They have helped many people overcome serious difficulties.

During this second week, continue with your relaxation techniques and follow them with visualizations. Each week during the recovery program, you will add new activities but also will continue the previous ones. You will build up a repertoire that will give you the strength and guidance to free yourself from compulsive shopping.

Week Three

Your goal in the third week is to bring order and control into your life by organizing your possessions and making lists of them.

Organizing Your Possessions

Organization is imperative to diminish the chaos in your life. An orderly physical environment is more conducive to a peaceful state of mind. Organizing your external world will help organize your inner world and lessen the anxious feelings that lead to compulsive shopping.

By organizing your possessions, you can use some of that anxious energy you usually spend in the stores. The guidelines here relate to organizing clothes closets, but they can be adapted to organizing any objects that you buy compulsively. For instance, if you buy too much makeup, you can write down all your lipsticks, mascaras, eyeliners, eyeshadows, base makeups, blushers, powders and perfumes. If you overspend on electronics, you can list each category of equipment and its specifics. If housewares are your weakness, organize and make lists of all items such as sheets, blankets, pillowcases, dishes, glasses, kitchen appliances. If lingerie is your weakness, list items such as pantyhose, stockings, teddies, nightgowns, slips and panties. Adapt the guidelines to suit your specific requirements.

Don't be overwhelmed by the amount of time and energy required to complete this project. Take it at your own pace. It may take days or even weeks to complete. Do what you can, with the goal of having your possessions completely organized and listed by the end of one month. If you think it would facilitate the process, enlist the help of a friend or your spouse.

Begin organizing your clothes by taking a large sheet of paper and labeling it with the current season. For example, if you're listing your winter wardrobe, write "Winter" in bold print on the top of each page. Label several pages, if you think you'll need them. Across the top of the page write the following column headings for women's winter garments: pants, skirts, dresses, suits, sweaters, blouses, outerwear, nightwear, footwear and accessories. For men's winter garments, write: pants, shirts, sweaters, sports clothes, suits, coats, nightwear, footwear and accessories. These are guidelines that you can adapt according to the categories that are most appropriate for you. Draw lines down the page to make columns for each category.

Go to your closets and drawers and organize the clothes for one season, according to categories and colors. For example, list all black pants, then pants of other colors, then sweaters and so forth. List and number each item under the appropriate heading. Try to list items of the same color directly underneath each other so you know how many similar items you have. You might want to add a descriptive word about articles of clothing that are in the same category and color, so you can differentiate between them. However, you might notice that differentiation is difficult and some of your purchases are very similar, as is common to many compulsive shoppers.

Be sure to look inside all your bags and boxes to be certain you've included everything. Set aside anything that you don't wear and enjoy. Give the surplus clothes to charity or to a relative or friend.

After you've finished the first season, follow the same procedure for the other seasons. If your clothing is in storage, go to your storage facility to make your lists, if possible. Modify the lists for each season. For example, include swimsuits under

"Summer." If this sounds like too much work, think of tackling it in sections. List one category of clothes for one season at first, and continue as time permits. Eventually you will complete the task and have—perhaps for the first time—a full understanding of how much you own.

This is one of the most courageous steps of your recovery process, because confronting the results of your shopping binges might make you profoundly uncomfortable. Do not be judgmental with yourself and do not be discouraged. Use the visualization and relaxation techniques to help you through this difficult period. Remember, you are bringing harmony and order into your life. The ancient Greeks believed that before the world as we know it existed, there was only chaos. Think of yourself as springing into life from out of the chaos.

Organizing your possessions will have very pleasant results. Every morning when you open your closet you will see a color-coordinated, organized array of clothing instead of confusion and disarray. You will start the day feeling more in control. Once you have conquered the initial organizational process, you will want to maintain it. Add any object that you purchase to your lists. Keep your closets and drawers tidy so you can always see at a glance what you already own and don't need to buy.

Keep the lists with you in an envelope. If you get the shopping urge, take them out and study them. This alone might discourage you from shopping. If you decide to go to the stores anyway, hand-carry the appropriate seasonal list with you. That way, if you're ready to buy your seventh cream-colored blouse or fifth gray belt, you can check the list and see how many you already have. This may break the momentum of the shopping frenzy. If it does, congratulate yourself. Remind yourself how much work and commitment it took to organize your belongings.

Week Four

• • • • • • • • • •

Your goal in the fourth week is to get in touch with your internal rhythms and your spending habits by keeping a daily checklist.

Daily Checklist

The daily checklist is a wonderful tool for self-discovery. It will enable you to chart your level of energy, your level of movement and your feelings. It will give you valuable clues as to when you are most vulnerable to the shopping compulsion.

Begin your checklist by writing the days of the week on the top of a piece of paper and dividing the page into squares for four weeks, just like a calendar. In fact, you can use a blank calendar page, if you wish. In each square, write: "E" for energy level, "M" for movement and "F" for feelings. Each day, write "L" for low, "M" for medium or "H" for high next to each "E," "M" and "F." The level of movement refers to how active you are that day. There will be fluctuations throughout the day, but one level will probably dominate and this is the one you should record. Also, with a red pen, write "S" for the days when you think a great deal about shopping and "S" with a circle around it for the days when you actually go shopping.

Create a comforting ritual around filling out your checklist. Do some relaxation and/or visualization techniques beforehand. Say your affirmations to yourself directly afterward. This will help bolster you if you are recording something disturbing.

After a month, study your chart carefully. Note what your levels of energy, movement and feelings were on the days when you went shopping or thought about it obsessively. Look for patterns, which will vary greatly. Many people do not have the energy to go shopping when they are low in all three categories, but when they begin to come out of the low period, the spending compulsion is strong. Some people are most vulnerable when their energy and movement levels are medium but their feelings are low. Others go shopping when their energy level is high, regardless of the other two factors. In this case, high energy is not necessarily a good thing, unless that energy is channeled into something more constructive than spending. Patterns may also involve the day of the week. Some compulsive shoppers have a tendency to binge on weekends, while others take to the stores in the middle of the week. These are just a few of the myriad of patterns that exist.

Some people take a few months to discover their pattern. Others realize that they don't have a particular pattern. Their compulsive spending is erratic. Even if you don't spot a pattern, continue keeping the checklist. One of the reasons for compulsive shopping is avoidance or denial of emotions. The checklist will give you a better understanding of your physiological and emotional rhythms and become a mirror of your life. Once you chart your internal rhythms, try to honestly discern what is causing your ups and downs. Then you can begin to take action to change whatever is bringing you down.

If you discover a pattern, try to catch yourself before succumbing to the shopping urge. On the days you are most likely to binge, delay shopping by using the methods discussed in the "Week Six" section.

Week Five

• • • • • • • • • • •

Your goal in the fifth week is to embark on a process of self-discovery by keeping a journal.

The Journal

If you want to make changes, you must take stock of yourself intellectually, emotionally, spiritually and physically. Writing is an invaluable tool for addressing and clarifying these dimensions. In your journal you can write about everyday events in your life and take a fresh look at them. You can let your mind wander into new definitions of yourself and your relationships. You can tap into your creativity and explore new ideas.

Before you begin writing in your journal, use one of the relaxation techniques. Then simply let it flow. Don't worry about spelling, grammar or style. Don't judge your words. They are for your eyes and benefit only. Try to write whatever comes into your mind. Take risks in your journal! Write in it as often as possible, every day if you can. Soon you will begin to think of writing as a pleasant release instead of a chore.

In addition to stream-of-consciousness writing, try writing about some of the following:

•

Your mother; your father; your siblings; children; marriage

•

Religion; spirituality; personal philosophy

•

What being a man or woman means to you

•

Love and affection; sex; romantic relationships

•

Friendship

•

Fantasies

What makes you happy

•

Your career, your goals

Another way to structure your journal is to answer core questions, such as the following:

•

Are your relationships fulfilling?
What can you do to improve them?

•

Are you happy in your work? Can you make
it more rewarding and enjoyable?

•

How would you like your life to be right now
if you could wave a magic wand?

•

What are your spiritual and moral values?

•

Are you neglecting any aspect of yourself?

•

What are some of the things you can do
to replace your addictive spending?

Answering these questions will help you uncover what you are ignoring or denying, allowing you to become clearer and more focused. You will discover a deeper state of knowing yourself than you have ever imagined.

Your goal is to write in your journal about five days a week, but you can work up to this level. Don't feel pressured to write a great deal. Consistency is more important than the length of the entry. Soon your journal will become a friend and confidante. This is a good way to practice expressing your feelings. Then you can take it a step further and express your feelings more with others.

Also remember to keep up your daily checklist (it only takes a few minutes a day). The journal and the checklist are natural companions. The journal will enable you to understand the meaning behind the notations you make on the checklist. Continue to organize your closets and make lists, but don't get angry with yourself if you slip behind a little. Keep up your morale with affirmations and visualizations. Remind yourself of the strength you have exhibited by embarking on the recovery process.

Week Six

Your goals in the sixth week are:

1. To learn techniques for delaying shopping.
2. To diminish the need to shop by cultivating alternative means of gratification.
3. To reduce the frequency, duration and intensity of your compulsive spending.

Delaying Shopping

When you become obsessed about shopping, think of what you will buy. Think about whether you need it. If it is not a vital necessity, try to put off shopping for at least one day. During the delay, frequently do visualization and relaxation techniques, and enjoy other gratifying activities. By the next day—or sometimes the next hour—your compulsion to buy may have passed.

Delaying shopping is an emotional exercise, and like a physical exercise, it may be uncomfortable or difficult. Try to bear the discomfort by telling yourself you are worthy of recovery and free, joyous living. Soon you will build your emotional muscles. When you're in a compulsive state, it is imperative to delay shopping until you're calmer and more rational. There are many ways you can do this.

Whenever you feel ripe for a shopping binge and/or are in an emotionally fragile state, call your buddy. Talk about your feelings. Ask your buddy to come over and visit with you, if possible. Perhaps you can plan to do something relaxing together, anything enjoyable that will keep you away from the stores. If it's a work day, plan to have lunch or an after-work snack with your buddy, another friend or a colleague at work. Plan ahead so that you don't head to the stores during these vulnerable times.

Alternative Gratification

There are many things you can do, without spending a great deal of money, to "reward" yourself for not shopping. You might want to spend a weekend day visiting a park, beach or lake. Being in a natural setting is very relaxing and replenishing, both physically and emotionally. Even if the weather is chilly, you can spend an hour or two taking a brisk walk outdoors. There is a beautiful, fascinating world outside of the stores!

Exercise is a wonderful way to dispel nervous energy. Sometimes you can improve your mood for the entire day by exercising for a short period of time. Choose a physical activity that you really enjoy. Don't bring a competitive or judgmental frame of mind to it—just play! You may want to take a class to learn a new form of exercise. That way, you can improve your social life as well as your body. The more you learn and grow, the less likely you are to resort to shopping for gratification.

You can expend the energy you waste shopping in a way that

benefits others as well as yourself. Exchange massages with your spouse. Spend extra time with your children or an elderly family member. Try volunteer work. It is a wonderful way to raise your self-esteem while helping others.

Also try to cultivate hobbies that you can enjoy alone. Read a good book, listen to inspiring music, try your hand at painting or any other hobby that attracts you. It might help to make a list of all the things you have thought you would like to try. Then pick out one or two of the most appealing ones, and try them. Once you are no longer a slave to shopping, you will have the energy and time to broaden your interests.

Reducing the Time and Money You Spend in Stores

Everyone has his or her own spending pattern. Some compulsive shoppers only spend once a month or less, but their spending habits are very destructive nonetheless. The other extreme involves the addicted spender who fritters away money almost every day. Most spending patterns fall somewhere between these two extremes.

If you shop frequently, it is important to cut down on the number of days you shop. The goal is to eliminate your trips to the stores when in a compulsive mode. If you cannot eliminate them completely, try to cut your shopping days in half. When you do go shopping, try to reduce the amount of time you spend in the stores by one-half. Plan enjoyable activities for yourself to fill up the time you would ordinarily spend in the stores. You may find that you're too busy to miss shopping!

When you do shop, decide beforehand what you are going to buy. Think about whether you need or even want the item, and check your lists to make sure you don't already own it. Do your relaxation exercises before shopping to ensure that you are as relaxed as possible. Once you have made your purchases, go home. Add the purchases to your lists and put them away in the appropriate places. Give yourself a pat on the back if you exerted a sense of control in the stores, but even if you shopped compulsively, be gentle with yourself. If you reduced the frequency, intensity or duration of your shopping, you have made progress. Whatever you do, do not be self-critical. Your developing awareness alone indicates that you are already progressing.

Week Seven

• • • • • • • • • •

Your goal in the seventh week is to eliminate chaos in your life by organizing your financial affairs.

Organizing Your Finances

An essential part of the recovery process involves organizing and handling your finances in a responsible manner. You will also need to confront and begin to deal with any debts you might have accrued.

The next chapter will supply specific advice on budgeting, saving, debt management, credit cards and other aspects of organizing your financial life. Once again, keep in mind that this step takes a great deal of resolve and bravery. Instead of belittling yourself if your finances are in chaos, commend yourself for taking the steps to straighten them out.

It is vital that you continue to do your visualizations, affirmations and relaxation techniques during the period of financial organization. These methods will help you to confirm your commitment and faith in recovery. Be sure to plan some pleasant outings and activities with friends during this week to alleviate your tension.

Week Eight

• • • • • • • • • •

Your goals in the eighth week are:
1. To reduce the number of your credit cards.
2. To take stock of your progress and confirm your commitment to recovery.

Reducing the Number of Credit Cards You Have

Your goal is to retain only one credit card, preferably one such as American Express, which must be paid in full at the end of each month. However, if the thought of getting rid of your cards fills you with tremendous anxiety, don't do it all at once.

First, do a creative visualization in which you picture yourself dispensing with your credit cards and feeling happy and strong afterward. Write down and repeat out loud the affirmation: "The less credit I have, the freer I am."

Then begin by cutting up the cards from one or two of your favorite department stores. Call up the stores immediately and tell them you want the cards canceled. Ask that they send you a written statement that your account is closed. If the store personnel try to dissuade you from closing the account, remember your resolve and firmly insist upon closing it. This is good practice in being assertive, a skill that you are now acquiring.

You might want to make an entry in your journal about how eliminating your credit cards makes you feel. Discuss your feelings with your friends and family, if it helps.

When you are ready, get rid of one of your major credit cards. Keep in touch with your feelings. If you are too frightened by the procedure, slow down and step up the activities introduced in previous weeks.

According to your pace, continue to eliminate your major credit cards and store cards. Eventually, you will have the strength to give up all your credit cards but one. The money you are spending will become real to you, and you will only buy what you can afford. Your anxiety, confusion and self-recrimination will be greatly reduced, as will your debts.

Coping with Withdrawal

You may experience a sense of painful withdrawal and/or depression at this point. These feelings can be the result of many factors. You might be angry at having to give up your addiction, even at the same time that you're feeling proud. Addiction is a part of you, albeit a destructive part, and it is a part of your persona that is dying. Mourning the loss of the old self is often part of the process of creating a new self. This mourning can lead to depression. For some people, this is a natural and essential part of the recovery process. Let yourself experience the sadness of letting go of a part of yourself that you knew so well. If you let yourself feel the sadness (an "alive" pain), the depression (a more numbed and morbid state) will lift. Talk to people who are close to you during this time, and seek professional counseling if you feel it would help.

Individual therapy in conjunction with this self-help program can facilitate your recovery. It can help you explore issues that underlie your shopping addiction and have deep ramifications for your life. If you feel that you need therapy but cannot afford it, you might check into community mental health clinics, where therapy is often much less costly.

Confirming Your Commitment

Take a look back at all you have achieved since beginning the recovery process. Most likely, you have already made tremendous progress toward defeating your shopping compulsion. If you have not made as much progress as you had hoped, don't let this defeat you. Rise to the challenge! Remember that everyone has his or her own recovery pace. Continue practicing the recovery activities. Each week, continue pursuing all the goals from previous weeks. Your awareness is changing, your life is expanding, and you're on the way to a more meaningful, fulfilled life. •

A budget is a road map to your future.—**Luther R. Gatling,** *President, Budget & Credit Counseling Services, Inc., New York City*

Chapter 8

Hands-On Financial Planning

This chapter offers specific advice for the many compulsive shoppers whose financial affairs are in chaos and who have accumulated debts. Even if you have no trouble keeping up with your bills, it will help you to read this chapter and apply the appropriate actions to your money matters. If your bills have always been handled by your spouse or a bookkeeper, accountant or secretary, now is the time to take an honest look at how much you spend. Even if you have not gone into debt, it will be valuable to confront the extent of your spending.

Taking control of your finances is an important aspect of taking control of your life. This step may seem frightening at first, but it will eventually reduce your anxiety and confusion. Be kind to yourself during the period of financial organization, and commend yourself for your persistence.

If possible, begin organizing your finances on a day when you have time and energy, do not have other pressing things on your mind and are feeling fairly calm. Start the day with one of the relaxation techniques, and try to remain as relaxed as possible. The calmer you remain, the more easily and quickly you will be able to deal with your financial matters.

Taking Inventory

Taking inventory is the first step toward gaining control over your financial life. If you are married, it is best to make this a joint inventory and include your spouses' income and expenses with your own.

Begin by writing down all your sources of income for a year, after taxes (net income). Include salaries, commissions, stock dividends, interest, monies from property, sales and business ventures, alimony and family trusts, if applicable. Add up these income sources, and divide the figure by 12 to arrive at an average monthly income. If you work freelance or your salary varies, divide the amount you earned last year by 12 to arrive at a monthly estimate.

On another sheet of paper, write down all your fixed monthly expenses: rent or mortgage payments, utilities, telephone, insurance and taxes. Then estimate your monthly expenses for the following categories:

- Food and drink (include the cost of eating and drinking outside the home).

- Household items such as home repairs, cleaning supplies, and professional help, if you have it. Add an approximate figure to cover the estimated cost of replacing essential home furnishings and appliances.

- Medical and dental bills, eyeglasses, prescriptions, vitamins, exercise classes and other health-related items.

- Transportation, including car maintenance, gasoline, tolls, bus, train, subway and taxi fares.

- Family expenses: if you have children, include their babysitting or day care, school supplies, tuition and other essentials.

- Charitable contributions and gifts, including any money you may regularly give to family or friends.

- An estimated amount to cover necessary new clothes and grooming items and services for you and your family.

- A recreation allowance to cover videos, movies, hobby equipment, sports, etc.

- A miscellaneous category for any other vital expenses.

If the category concerns one or more of the items you buy compulsively, do not write down how much you have been spending; write down a reasonable amount that you can afford to spend. For example, if you're a compulsive clothes buyer who is single, you may be spending $2,000 a month or more in the clothes and grooming category, but your estimate should be considerably less. Remember, this is not your budget, nor is it expected to be exact. It is simply a way to find out where you stand monetarily.

Add up all your expenses, then subtract this figure from the figure representing your total monthly income. Let's call the result your "surplus money." This is the money you have available to repay your debts.

This next step is distressing but inevitable. Don't postpone it. Get it over with and you'll feel better afterward. Write down a list of your debts: whom the money is owed to, the amounts due and the due dates. Include debts to friends, relatives, stores, credit cards, car and appliance payments, banks or other loan agencies. Then total up the debts.

Handling Your Debts

If your debts do not seem overwhelming, set up a repayment schedule based on your available surplus money. If you've been neglecting certain debts, call those creditors and honestly explain your situation. Trying to avoid your creditors does not make them forget your debts; it only creates a hostile relationship. If you make an effort to repay at least some of the debt on a regular basis, many creditors will be reasonable about the rate of payment. Write a letter to confirm any repayment schedules you have discussed with them verbally, and keep a copy of the letter for yourself. Then stick to your schedule faithfully. Doing this will greatly enhance your self-confidence and self-esteem, as it diminishes your indebtedness.

There is an alternative way to handle your debts, if you have the financial resources. In addition to paying the minimum payment on all your bills each month, you can try to pay the smallest bill in full. This will enable you to get rid of one creditor each month and give you a sense of satisfaction and progress.

If your surplus money is a small or non-existent amount, your debts seem too great to handle, you are considering bankruptcy, or you are confused, seek professional financial counseling.

The National Foundation for Consumer Credit is a non-profit organization that is affiliated with 285 agencies throughout the country. These agencies charge a nominal fee of $50 or less to help debtors with budgeting guidelines, paycheck analysis, credit and loan information, setting up repayment schedules and dealing with creditors.

To find out the location of the agency nearest you, write or call:
The National Foundation for Consumer Credit
8701 Georgia Avenue
Silver Springs, Maryland 20910
(301) 589-5600

Debt Consolidation

When faced with the chaos of many creditors, some people turn to debt consolidation: borrowing one lump sum to pay back all the other debts. This is hazardous for several reasons. First of all, many of these private "debt adjusters" or "consolidators" are unscrupulous. They charge excessive amounts of interest, leave the debtor little money to live on, or fail to pay back the creditors as promised.

However, even if you borrow from a bank, pension fund or other reputable source, consolidation can be dangerous if you are not fully recovered from the shopping addiction. Consolidation enables you to have open credit once again, leaving you vulnerable to sinking deeper into debt. Also, you might need to spend some time each month dealing with your creditors yourself, as a reminder of the serious nature of your shopping compulsion.

Credit Clinics

If you seek advice regarding your debts, be careful to approach a legitimate consumer service and not a private "credit clinic," "credit doctor" or "credit repair shop."

Luther R. Gatling, president of the Budget and Credit Counseling Services, Inc., a non-profit corporation licensed by the New York State Banking Department, offers these words of warning: "Credit clinics or credit repair shops are a total ripoff and have been outlawed in many states. You should always check with the Better Business Bureau and the State Banking Department, because many of them are not authorized and are just loan sharks. They also 'flim-flam' people by telling them they can restore their credit ratings when they cannot. Negative information appears on credit reports for a seven-year period of time, with the exception of New York, which deletes the information after five years if the debt is satisfied."

Linda Barbanel, MSW, a New York City psychotherapist and educator specializing in money issues, has this to say: "Credit doctors negotiate with your creditors, but they don't teach you how to manage your money. This sets people free to overspend again."

When you are seeking professional help, be careful to distinguish between these credit clinics, which promise to take away all your problems, and legitimate counseling agencies that teach you how to handle your finances better.

Many people are concerned about having negative information on their credit-rating report. Your credit rating should not be one of your chief concerns at this time. It is better to devote your efforts toward learning to live within your budget—without a great deal of credit. Negative information on a credit report can have a positive effect. It can prevent you from getting credit, which might tempt you to overspend.

Remember Your Rights

Many addicted spenders panic when they are faced with large debts. This causes anxiety, which can lead to a shopping binge. There is no reason to succumb to panic. There are no longer debtors' prisons in the United States. There are also laws to protect you against your creditors.

The Fair Debt Collection Practices Act applies to all debt collectors, from family members to whom you owe money to collection agencies to corporate collection departments. It states that debt collectors can call you only between the hours of 8 a.m. and 9 p.m., unless you agree otherwise. They are not allowed to call you at work if your employer does not approve. They may contact other persons only for the express purpose of discovering your whereabouts.

You can write letters to debt collectors to tell them to stop trying to reach you. After they receive the written notification, they are allowed to contact you only for two reasons: to inform you that they are taking a specific action or to tell you that they won't be contacting you again.

If you feel you are being harassed by debt collectors, remind them of your rights. If they persist in disregarding the Fair Debt Collection Practices Act, you can consider taking legal action and filing suit against them. For more information regarding this law, check the phone book for the branch of the Federal Trade Commission nearest you.

If you have been threatened with wage garnishment by a debt collector, familiarize yourself with the Federal Wage Garnishment Law, which limits the amount of wages an employer can withhold to pay off creditors. Branches of the U.S. Labor Department can be contacted for further information.

The Truth in Lending Act protects you if you are seeking a loan. It requires lenders to disclose information such as: the total finance charge; due dates and amounts of payments; penalties for late payments; minimum payments required; and the periodic rate used to compute finance charges on open-end credit accounts. Take full advantage of this protective law by getting information in writing from your lender, reading it carefully, and consulting someone knowledgeable to make sure you understand the terms.

If your debts are too enormous to handle, you might consider another right provided by law: filing for bankruptcy.

Bankruptcy

"Congress, through the Bankruptcy Act, allows any American a fresh start through bankruptcy," says Luther R. Gatling. However, bankruptcy should be considered as a last alternative because it has severely negative connotations in our society and can lower self-esteem. If you are personally involved with any of your creditors or co-signers of loans, bankruptcy can adversely affect your relationships with them. It also is the most damaging information you can have on your credit report, and it remains there for seven to ten years.

If you are considering bankruptcy, consult a reputable counseling service or attorney to determine whether it is a necessary step. If you, your advisors and family members agree that bankruptcy is the only way out of debt, you have two alternatives.

You can file a Chapter XIII petition, also known as the Wage Earner Plan. Under this plan, you, your creditors, a referee and a federal judge work out an installment repayment plan. Over the next three years, you must make payments to a government trustee, who pays your creditors. The plan can also be extended for a five-year period, if the court mandates, and can involve either a total or partial repayment of debts. This plan protects most of your assets; however, it does go on record as a bankruptcy and stays on your credit record for seven years.

The other alternative is filing a Chapter VII petition for straight bankruptcy. Under this petition, all your assets—except for certain exemptions, which vary from state to state—are collected by the court. The court liquidates your assets and the proceeds are dispersed to your creditors, thereby ending your responsibility for the debts. This type of bankruptcy stays on your credit record for 10 years.

Budgets and Savings

Maintaining a budget and saving money is part of the maintenance program for recovered compulsive shoppers. It is one of the best ways to avoid debts. To many people, the word "budget" has a negative, punitive connotation. Try to make your attitude more positive by thinking of a budget as a tool to help you overcome compulsive spending and make your life easier in general. A budget can lessen your anxiety and give you a new sense of security and control. If you follow the guidelines of the budget, you will experience greater financial and emotional freedom.

"Everyone has different fantasies about what money can do for them," says Linda Barbanel. "And everybody has a different money style." It's important that your budget fit your money style and your lifestyle. If you are a non-conformist who gets nervous when things are too structured, keep your budget somewhat loose and flexible. If you enjoy planning ahead and having an organized pattern to your days, a more specific budget is right for you. There are many excellent books on budgeting. However, don't feel that you have to stick to the experts' advice. If you prefer, you can make up your own budget plan.

If you're married, you should work with your spouse on preparing your budget. Some couples prefer to have separate budgets, with each contributing to categories like rent and utilities, but with separate allowances for personal items and entertainment. This can give you a feeling of autonomy and freedom. However, even if you choose to have separate budgets, it is a good idea to have your spouse there for the initial budgeting session. Work together to iron out any disagreements about spending priorities that come up and make the necessary compromises.

You might want to use the categories of expenses in the "Taking Inventory" section of this chapter to work out your budget. Whatever you choose, remember to add this category: savings. You may have never started a savings account before. You may have depleted it during shopping binges. Or you may already have substantial savings. Whatever the case, part of your recovery plan involves learning to save money. It doesn't have to be a great deal. If you are in debt, it may be only $5 a week. The important thing is not the amount, but the consistent pattern of saving.

Saving will raise your self-esteem and give you faith in your self-control. Linda Barbanel suggests the following affirmations to help you save: "I deserve the best. I am going to be my own parent and plan for the future. I like myself and take care of myself."

Credit Cards and Checks

Perhaps you have been relying so heavily on credit cards and checks that your cash flow is not real to you, and you have no idea where your money goes. The following exercise is meant for those who have serious budgeting and/or credit-card problems. It is a concrete way of seeing where your money goes. If you do it once or twice, it will leave a lasting impression on you about the reality of your expenses.

Label envelopes with the following: rent, utilities, telephone, insurance, food, transportation, child expenses, debt payments, savings and miscellaneous (any other fixed expenses you have each month). Cash your paycheck and put the money into the appropriate envelopes. Put whatever money is left over into another envelope and mark it "shopping." For those of you who don't have a monthly paycheck, put a specified amount (not too much) into the shopping envelope.

During the month that you do this exercise, leave all your credit cards and checks behind when you go shopping. Take the "shopping" envelope and spend only the cash inside. This will be a dramatic change for you and a valuable experience in shopping with "real" money.

Although checks can be used to pay bills, it is advisable to go shopping without checkbook in hand until you are fully recovered. You might feel naked without your checkbook at first, but soon you will learn to feel comfortable without the false sense of security that checks provide.

The previous chapter discussed how to wean yourself from dependency on credit cards, a vital aspect of your recovery program. Once you have garnered the strength to eliminate all your cards but one, try to leave even that one at home when you go shopping. When applications or unsolicited new cards arrive in the mail, tear them up and throw them out. As the anti-drug slogan goes: "Just say no!" •

I finally realized
that someone could
really love me for
who I was and not
what I wore.—**Kim**

Chapter 9

Support Groups for Shopaholics

The Shopaholics Limited® groups in New York City are composed of six to ten compulsive shoppers who gather each week to give each other support and guidance in overcoming their spending problems. The groups are run by a professional psychotherapist who helps group members confront underlying issues, when appropriate. The psychotherapist guides the group through relaxation and visualization exercises and creates the structure for the meetings. The members share their experiences and support each other through the recovery process.

Why Support Groups Work

It is extremely comforting not to feel alone with a problem and to meet others who have shared the experiences of addiction, from the euphoria to the shame. The group provides a place where people can let down their defenses and allow their feelings to emerge without fear of judgment. It offers a supportive atmosphere for self-discovery and growth. Sharing their innermost fears and hopes, the members of the group often become very close. In a sense, the group becomes an extended family and provides a feeling of community, which many shopaholics sorely lack.

The very nature of the support group is healing. Sharing one's addiction eases the terrifying sense of being alone and out of control. Helping other group members raises both parties' self-esteem. When people are nurturing and gentle with others, they learn to be that way toward themselves. When they care for others with the same problem, it makes it easier to accept themselves. Being linked to others in this manner helps fill the void of intimacy that many feel. It also opens the door to deeper communication, improving all relationships.

The buddy system is an inherent part of the support group. The members call each other when they feel the urge to binge, and/or feel depressed, confused or upset for any reason. Having someone to talk to is comforting, and the members encourage and support each other during difficult times. Many group members have helped each other stay away from the stores by having lunch together during work days. Some have developed lasting, deep friendships that expand their lives.

Support groups provide hope. The group is an ongoing event, with new members entering at different times. The new members meet people who have conquered their addictions or progressed a great deal toward recovery. These "older" members are inspiring examples of recovery and can offer practical advice.

I feel that all compulsive behaviors, from alcoholism to overspending, are dealt with most effectively and quickly in a support-group setting. However, private psychotherapy is often an important adjunct. The support group works on the specific compulsion, while the therapy can explore underlying reasons in an in-depth manner.

Opening Up and Exploring

Before new members join the group, I have one or two lengthy telephone conversations with them to answer questions they may have and to provide background information. In spite of our conversations, meeting the group for the first time and talking about the addiction inspires a mixture of emotions: awkwardness, embarrassment, shame, self-consciousness, shyness or ambivalence about being there. However, the group is structured in such a way that these feelings are quickly dispelled.

Meetings usually are held in a private home once a week for 90 minutes. This informal atmosphere is conducive to relaxation. At the beginning of each meeting, members spend a few moments mingling and talking. This establishes a bond in a low-key natural fashion. Everyone then lies down, and the psychotherapist guides them through the progressive relaxation exercise described in Chapter Seven.

"I couldn't believe it the first time I did the relaxation," said Anne. "I had no idea how hyped up I was until I tried to relax." The relaxation method taught Anne to get in touch with her body. "I used to get a lot of tension headaches, probably because I was holding in so much anger. Now that I've learned to let go, the headaches are much less frequent."

Richard found himself falling asleep during the relaxation exercise. It's not unusual for people who have been very tense to fall asleep when "given permission" to relax. Their bodies, no longer "on alert," succumb to what they really need—rest and sleep.

Jamie began using the relaxation techniques to help herself fall asleep. "I had trouble sleeping ever since my divorce. But now I can put myself right out by doing the relaxation exercise. It's better than a lullaby." Being well-rested also aids recovery, because it makes it easier to cope with the demands of the day.

After the relaxation, the group often does a guided visualization, which varies from session to session. For example, members are asked to visualize a time when they felt very sure of themselves, their behavior and thoughts. They are reminded to pay attention to exactly how their bodies felt at that time. Afterward, they share their experiences during the visualization exercise. They are always given the option to keep their experiences private, but most members choose to share them.

"I felt the strength in my legs," Marsha said during a session. "I felt very tall and strong. I thought of myself as one of those mythological Amazon women." She evoked this feeling several weeks later when she faced a meeting with her estranged husband to discuss their finances. "I felt weak in the knees when I was waiting for him. Then I remembered the Amazon feeling. It enabled me to feel strong and act strong, which I had always had trouble doing around him. I didn't buckle under. I told him what I needed and stood by it."

At some meetings, the group is guided through a fantasy. During Claudia's first week in the group, the guided fantasy concluded with everyone giving themselves a gift. During the discussion afterward, Claudia said, "I gave myself a statue of a woman. But it was strange, there was a rope around her chest."

At this point, I intervened. First, I asked her if she was willing to work. When she said yes, I asked her to stand up and "be" the statue—experience the rope around her chest. "Can you take it off and unbind yourself?" I asked.

She did that easily, but then she exclaimed, "There's another rope around my ankles. I can't stand on my own two feet!" For Claudia, this was an epiphany—a moment of revelation and sudden clarity. Every detail of her dependency rushed into her head: her dependence on men for validation; her dependence on those to whom she owed money; her dependence on shopping and on credit cards.

To everyone's surprise, she came in the following week with all of her credit cards, except her American Express. She said she wanted to cut them up but needed the support of the group while she did it. It normally takes people more time to be ready to do this, but Claudia's revelation was a great motivating force. She was ready. Ceremoniously, Claudia took a pair of scissors and cut up the cards to a round of applause from the delighted group. Each time someone in the group makes progress, it is shared by all the other members. Each individual triumph is a triumph for everyone.

After these exercises, new group members relate their stories. They generally share background information, such as whether they are married or single, where they live and work, and their shopping history. This includes how often they spend and how much, where and when they shop, what they buy, how they feel when they shop and what brought them to the group. The new members share only as much as is comfortable for them. They are never pushed to do or say anything they're not ready for.

This is a crucial point for new members. At this time they decide whether or not to make a commitment to recovery. Occasionally, someone is not willing to bear the discomfort and decides not to return to the group. Usually, however, some of the initial shame is dissipated because of the reactions of other members. There are empathetic smiles and nods and comments such as, "I used to do that," and "I know what you mean."

When Kim joined the group, she told about buying a $400 leather skirt, then going home and finding three almost identical ones in her closet.

"I once bought three black wool coats in the same season," said Claudia. "Practically the only thing that was different about them were the buttons."

Kim laughed, relief shining in her eyes. "Claudia, you look so great and so together, it's a relief finding out that you could do crazy things like me," she said.

"I think we all do crazy things," said Denise. "I bought a $150 outfit for my daughter that she grew out of in three months!"

"I bought clothes that didn't even fit me, just because I saw someone else in a club wearing them," said Brad.

After the new members tell their stories, each person is asked to pay a nominal fee for the session. They are reminded to notice what they are thinking and what they are experiencing in their bodies as they pay. This enables them to cultivate conscious spending, becoming aware of the different ways one can feel while spending. Some members feel badly at first, guilty that they have an addiction they must pay to treat. Some feel neutral, lacking the chaotic feelings that accompany their compulsive spending. Many feel good. "This is the first time I'm using money to help myself," "I feel in control, I don't feel confused," and "I feel hopeful," are characteristic comments.

Sharing the Shopping Week

After the payment ritual, group members talk about their shopping experiences that week, discussing any patterns they found on their checklists and other relevant information.

Lisa was a fritterer who went shopping almost every day, so she was given the task of going shopping only twice a week, on Tuesdays and Saturdays. Having "permission" to go shopping twice a week was less threatening to her than the idea of stopping "cold turkey." She found she was able to adhere to this schedule, and this made her feel more in control. On her sixth week in the group, she told us, "I didn't shop at all this week. I finally realized that I wasn't getting anything substantial when I went shopping all the time. I was buying a bunch of worthless junk. I decided I'd rather save up my shopping allowance and buy something special, something I really needed."

"That's a great idea," said Jamie. "I stopped buying all those housewares for a couple of weeks, and then I treated myself to a nice business suit. It felt good to buy something I really needed for a change."

"Something I really need is clothes to wear on dates. But I spend so much on workout clothes, I don't have enough money left over," said Marie. "So I still end up feeling like I don't look good when I go out, even after all the time I spend getting in shape."

"I think you put too great an emphasis on how you look," said Richard.

"Oh come on, all guys want a woman with a great body," said Marie.

"Men don't only care how a woman looks. They also care how she feels about herself," said Richard.

"I have to be really thin, or I don't feel good about myself. But I guess the truth is, I never feel thin enough—or good enough," said Marie.

At his fourth meeting, David admitted he had had a bad week.

"I met this new girl, a gorgeous model. I really wanted to impress her, so I bought her $50 worth of roses when I picked her up for our first date. I took her to this new restaurant everyone's talking about, had champagne, the works. The tab was about $300."

"Do you see any patterns in your checklist, David?" I asked.

He looked at it. "High energy, high movement, high feelings almost every day," he said. "Well, I guess 'high' isn't so hot for me, because about two days after that date I went out with some of my old college buddies. It was supposed to be just for a drink, but then we got hungry and had dinner in the place. I picked up the whole tab. I realized afterward that my stomach was in knots."

"David, I asked you to call me if you were in that kind of situation," said Richard. "Why didn't you?"

"I just didn't think of it. Maybe next time," he said.

"At least you were aware that your stomach was in knots," said Marsha. "You're learning to listen when your body speaks."

"That's important," said Olivia. "The other day I went to Macy's because I needed some new pantyhose, and I started getting that feeling in my body—very jumpy like my heart was racing, agitated..."

"That feeling reminds me of the kind of rush I used to get when I was into cocaine," said Kim. "Like you want to race somewhere, but you don't know where."

"Well, I've never done cocaine, but when I get that feeling in my body, I know where to race—out of the store!" said Olivia.

During her fifth week in the group, Anne went on a serious binge. She was so ashamed that she considered skipping the meeting, so as not to have to tell the others. But her commitment to recovery gave her the strength to come forth with her story. "I had a terrible week," she said, "the usual job pressure and then coming home to more problems. Josh was always a pretty good student. Suddenly, this semester, he comes home with 'F's' and 'D's' on his report card because he's apparently been cutting class. He's hanging out with a new group of kids who look like a bunch of druggies."

"Have you tried to talk to him about it?" asked Marsha.

"Sure I tried. But he won't talk to me. He just shrugs and says 'I dunno' or 'I don't care' to everything. Then he goes up to his room and blasts that heavy metal music. It drives me nuts."

"Maybe your husband can get through to him," said David.

"It can be hard to get your husband to do his share," said Denise.

"When he tries to talk to Josh, Jeff just gets so frustrated he ends up screaming. Then he comes down and starts in on me. 'What kind of mother are you, bringing up a kid like this?' he asked me one day last week. I was so upset I couldn't stand being in that house one more minute. I got in the car and drove straight to the mall. I knew it was wrong. I knew I was being compulsive. I knew it went against everything we learn here, but I had to do it. I didn't have my credit cards because I got rid of those, but I did have my checkbook. I bought over $2000 worth of clothes. Of course I felt absolutely sick about it afterward. The checks were from our joint account, and Jeff's going to explode when he finds out."

"Can you take the stuff back?" asked Lisa.

"Well, about five hundred dollars worth is from a place where I can get a cash refund, and I guess I can get store credit for the rest."

"Then take it back. You can use up the store credit slowly, when you really need something," said Lisa.

"I guess I can do that. But I still hate myself for buying it," said Anne.

"We've all done things like that," said Claudia. There were

affirmative nods from other members of the group. "As time goes on, those episodes will become less frequent."

"And eventually they'll stop happening," said Lisa.

"The important thing is to stay calm and be kind to yourself," I said. "It was a serious binge and it's good that you acknowledge that. But what good does it do to beat yourself up over it now? Will that make you shop less or more?"

"If your family upsets you, remember you can call me any-time," said Olivia. "I've raised teen-agers myself, and I know how they can be."

"Me too," said Marsha. "They certainly can be impossible, but it really helps to talk. Call me next time."

Anne smiled as she soaked up the empathy and support emanating toward her. As often happens, it was not merely the dialogue that was helpful, but also the close-knit feeling of the group. They shared a few quiet moments of healing love and mutual support.

The Group Discussion

Sometimes, sharing the shopping week takes up the entire meet-ing, especially if a new member is present or if someone is facing a special problem. However, most meetings include a discussion with a specific theme. Topics are similar to the ones suggested for your journal writing. The concern with Anne's familial problems prompted the theme for that meeting to be the age-old question: Love, is it worth it?

"Sometimes I wonder. I fantasize about how easy my life would be if I didn't have to worry about Jeff and the kids," said Anne.

Kim shook her head. "You're lucky to have a family, no matter how hard it is. Without a family, there's always emptiness in your life."

"It's true, there's nothing like a family. Nothing in the world makes me feel as good as looking at my baby," said Denise.

"My family is the most precious thing in the world to me," said Olivia.

"I still feel that way about my children, but I'm not sure I do about my husband. I don't know if it's worth giving up what I want to do with my life in order to keep him," said Marsha.

"I really miss being married," said Jamie. "I hope I get married again, but none of the men I meet seem interested in a serious relationship. If I start to bring up something real, like talking about my kids or something, they shy away."

"I feel like a Barbie doll sometimes," said Marie. "Like men just want to play with me and toss me away and play a different game. I wish I knew what I was doing wrong, because I'd love to be married."

"Maybe it's the way you present yourself," said Marsha. "Maybe you give the impression of only being after a good time yourself."

"That's easy for you to say because you haven't been in the singles scene. Men do not want to listen to anyone else's problems," said Kim.

"I think it goes both ways," said Richard. "Sometimes I try to talk to a girl I meet at a party about something serious, and she thinks I'm getting too heavy."

"I feel that if I tell a woman my problems, she's going to think I'm weak or neurotic. Woman want a big strong guy who has no worries," David said.

"Not all women want a macho type. Most women are very understanding and helpful if you open up," said Claudia.

"That's one of the nice things about being married," Olivia said. "You can stop playing those games and be yourself."

"I decided I'm going to be myself with women, and if they

can't handle it, they're not right for me," said Richard.

"That's great, but it has to go both ways. You have to be willing to listen to them too. Some men want you to be their shrink, but they don't have any time for your problems," Jamie said. "There has to be give and take."

"Do you think it ever really works that way?" asked Kim.

"I think it's important that we believe it can. If you keep telling yourself, 'men are no good,' you'll keep attracting the wrong men. If you believe that you deserve a healthy relationship, you're more likely to get one," I said.

"I guess that's why I hope to get Jeff into therapy. I keep believing that we can make our marriage work because the love is still there," said Anne.

"As long as the love is there, you can get through anything," said Olivia. "Frank and I have certainly been through our ups and downs, but we know we love each other and that keeps us together."

"Love certainly isn't easy and it isn't simple," said Lisa, "but it's worth it."

"I wish I knew what everyone was talking about," said Brad. "I don't because I've never been in love. I'd like to be, but I don't even meet anyone, let alone fall in love."

"Oh I meet plenty of people—and I fall in love—but they never do," said Marie.

After the discussion winds down, the group shares a few moments of deep breathing and quiet reflection. Then they are left with a positive message such as this: "Remember you've made a commitment to yourself. You're on the right path. And we are here for you."

The Group Members' Recoveries

You've gotten to know some of the members of the Shopaholics Limited® group—learned about their shopping habits and their underlying issues. Now you will see how they have progressed toward recovery, and in many cases, completely freed themselves from their shopping addiction.

Olivia

Certain members of the group naturally gravitate toward each other and form deep friendships. Olivia became close friends with Marsha. Because she had been in the program longer, she helped Marsha through many rough moments. Helping her friend increased Olivia's self-esteem. As she cultivated her nurturing side, she began to feel less like a "lost child" and more like an effective strong woman.

By assisting Marsha and other members of the group, Olivia discovered the fulfillment that comes from helping others. She began to contemplate doing some type of volunteer work. She found her niche when Marsha took her on expeditions to the city to visit galleries and artists' studios. "Marsha took me to neighborhoods where I had never been before. I was shocked to see so many homeless people living on the streets," said Olivia. "I decided to volunteer for an organization that helps the homeless. It makes me feel so good to know that I'm doing something worthwhile with my time, instead of wasting it in the stores. Once I became involved in volunteer work, I started to become more aware of all the deprived people in the world. So now each week I take some money that I would have spent on shopping and give it to a charity. It gives me much more satisfaction than spending it on myself ever did."

Olivia has met new friends through her job who involve her in social activities that keep her away from the stores. Although she still does not like to be alone, she now finds it easier to fill up her days without shopping. She tries to limit her shopping to one day a week and always checks her lists before she goes. She still feels nervous in the stores, but now she has the strength to walk out when she feels agitated. "I find that deep breathing really helps," she said. "I'll do it right in the store if I need to. Or I'll say the affirmations to myself."

Marsha

In the last month, Marsha had one serious spending spree. "It was the start of a new art season, and I knew I would be going to a lot of openings. I suddenly felt so insecure about not looking right that I went out and bought nine expensive outfits."

The group helped get her back on track by reminding her that she didn't have to shop her way into acceptance. That was an old tape that she could now stop playing. "I also felt better when the group reminded me that I used to spree like that once or twice a week," said Marsha.

Marsha finds the journal to be an excellent tool for self-discovery. "Writing is helping me find out who I am and where I want to be," she said. She is still separated from her husband and is uncertain whether she wants reconciliation. "In the meantime, I've been on a few dates and I must say, it's exciting to spend time with men who see me as an intelligent person in my own right."

Marsha moved from her first job into an assistant managerial position in another gallery. She is taking graduate courses in art administration. "I originally went back to school in order to further my career opportunities, and I find I'm enjoying every minute of it. I love learning! A side benefit is that between work and school, I hardly have time to think about shopping."

Brad

Brad initially joined the group at his parents' insistence. They realized that he was spending far more than he should and recognized that he had a shopping compulsion. Although he tried to deny this, his parents kept after him until he reluctantly agreed to join the group.

Perhaps because he did not join of his own volition, Brad remained in the denial stage for longer than most members of the group. Finally, after about six weeks, he was able to open up and admit that he went shopping to assuage his lack of self-confidence, his loneliness and his frequent depressions.

"When I was a kid, I thought that no one liked me because I was fat. When I lost the weight, I thought that everything would be great; I'd have lots of friends and girlfriends. But no one seemed to notice or care. So I thought the way to get them to notice and like me was to look really, really good," said Brad. "I bought all these great clothes, but no matter how much I spent, I was still lonely."

The friendship and support of members of the group was a nourishing experience for Brad. With their help, he came to realize that "clothes don't make the man," and also that there are better places to meet people than in the superficial atmosphere of nightclubs.

He began going to seminars and classes on human potential and spiritual matters. This was the missing component that Brad discovered had been lacking in his life. This involvement had several benefits. He expanded his inner self, and he met open, warm people and developed new friendships. As his world opened up, his preoccupation with appearance faded. He no longer felt the compulsion to overspend. "I realize now that it matters more who I am and what I think than how I look," said Brad.

David

David became aware of his need to please and impress others. "I decided to do something about it," he said. "I told my friends that

I wanted to see some of my money wind up in my savings account. I laughed and said, 'So I won't be pickin' up the tab anymore, guys.' I felt nervous. I guess on some level I was afraid they wouldn't like me anymore, but they still did and that made me feel good." David started to believe that people could like him for himself. This increased his self-esteem and paved the way for deeper relationships.

He is still a perfectionist in his business, but he is learning to cut down his hours by delegating authority to others. He hired a bookkeeper and is thinking of hiring other helpers to alleviate his work load. "I guess you could say I'm working on not being such a workaholic," said David.

Although he still overspends, usually on dates, he has cut down his entertainment expenses considerably. This has given him more money to invest in his own business and money to start a savings account. He has not yet found the courage to dispense with his credit cards, but the group is supporting him and he hopes to do so soon.

Claudia

The dramatic statue visualization catapulted Claudia's recovery forward. She was able to cut up her credit cards much sooner than most people and was deeply determined to free herself from the bonds of compulsive shopping.

"Organizing my closets was another great motivator," she said. "I could hardly believe how much I had. I gave a lot away to my sister and my friends. It felt nice to give for a change. But I felt even better when I could pay them back the money I owed them."

Despite her determination, Claudia had been a compulsive shopper for many years, and it was a difficult habit to break. She overspent at least once a month for the first few months. Still, it was not as out-of-control as previously. She checked her lists before she went and took them with her. She tried everything on and considered her purchases carefully, as opposed to her old habit of buying directly off the rack.

"The group and all the techniques I learned enable me to look at people in a fresh light. I now realize that a woman can be beautiful and desirable even if she doesn't have twenty designer cocktail dresses. I began to think about what was truly important in life and what wasn't. Now I realize that you cannot buy the most important things."

Although she had never admitted it to herself, marriage and family were important to Claudia. She entered psychotherapy to work on the issues that had caused her to become involved with unavailable men. The combination of the group and therapy yielded results quite rapidly. Claudia began dating men who weren't married or otherwise unavailable, men with whom marriage could be a reality.

By her sixth month in the group, Claudia was a recovered compulsive shopper. She had paid her debts and set up a budget for herself, with a specific shopping allowance. However, she chose to come to the group for another eight months, because she appreciated the support and enjoyed helping others over the hurdles.

Jamie

It took Jamie about three months to begin believing in the possibility of her own recovery. She was so accustomed to thinking negatively about herself, it was hard for her to have any faith. "It wasn't until I saw people with really bad problems get better that I began to think maybe I could make it too," she said.

Jamie was also resistant to incorporating the self-help techniques into her life. "I had no trouble with the things like the checklist and the organizing, but I had a hard time with the visualizations and affirmations. I've always been a pragmatic type, and I had no faith. Then someone in the group suggested some books on creative visualization and positive thinking. I found they were helpful. When I started to be more open to the techniques, they started working for me."

Jamie went to a financial counseling service, where they helped her work out a budget and a debt-repayment schedule. "Up to that point, I was still spending too much, but the schedule and the budget gave me a definite goal," said Jamie. "I learned that if I stuck to them, I could pay off my debts in five months, and if I saved a certain amount, I could afford to move with the kids into a garden apartment in another four months. That gave me a definite goal and motivated me to stay away from the stores. I started doing visualizations where I would picture being in a nice new apartment with my kids and a man who really cared about us. Whenever I would get that old shopping urge, I would conjure up that picture, and it would keep me from binging—usually. Sometimes I would go shopping anyway, but I would play a little trick on myself. I would only go to stores where I could return the items for cash. That way, the next day, after I'd done the relaxation exercises and all and was feeling back to normal, I could return the stuff if necessary." Many compulsive shoppers need this type of safety net in the early stages of recovery.

Denise

Denise first joined the group primarily because it was a chance to get out of the house and discuss her problems with sympathetic peers. She found it very comforting to have people who understood not only her shopping compulsion, but also her problems with motherhood.

"As painful as it was, I had to admit that my overspending had to do with my ambivalence about being a mother. On one hand, I love Crystal so much, and I wanted to be with her all the time. On the other hand, I resented being stuck in the house with her all day," said Denise. "I felt guilty for feeling this way, so I would buy things for her to try and make me feel better."

This revelation paved the way to Denise's recovery. She came to understand that it was imperative to her psychological well-being for her to work outside the home. Denise and Jamie, who had become supportive "buddies" and close friends, worked out a plan to share the expense of a baby-sitter. This allowed Denise to work part time as a freelance nurse. She found the work satisfying and also preferred not being totally dependent on her husband's income.

At first, Denise felt guilty about leaving her baby with the baby-sitter. This guilt propelled her to go on occasional shopping sprees for the child. The group helped her deal with these feelings and her underlying conflicts about motherhood. She gradually learned to accept that she needed to work in order to feel complete, and this did not mean she was a bad mother. As she became more secure in her mothering as well as her life outside the home, she no longer felt compelled to shop excessively.

"Now I'm saving money for my daughter's future, instead of wasting it on things she's too young to enjoy," said Denise.

Marie

When Marie's parents made plans to sell their house and move to a retirement community, she was forced to confront her spending habits. Unless she got them under control, she would never be able to afford her own apartment, which would soon be a necessity. So she joined the group hoping for a quick fix for her shopping addiction.

Marie shied away from introspection, so the depth of the group's discussions was a very new experience for her. "I came into the group just to learn how to stop shopping so much, but then I discovered there was a lot more to it. There were a lot of deep problems I had been keeping inside that were making me shop. I guess I just wasn't ready to deal with these problems."

Marie decided to leave the group after two months. She said she had stopped compulsive spending, so there was no need for her to continue coming to sessions. Knowing that there were many unresolved issues in Marie's life, I felt she still needed the support of the group and encouraged her to stay, but she insisted that she was ready to leave.

Unfortunately, it proved true that Marie was far from ready. Not only did she begin overspending again, but she developed another addiction: bulimia. Her obsession with her weight and appearance made her susceptible to this eating disorder, and once she was no longer living in the controlled environment of her parents' home, she began a destructive cycle of binging and purging.

Bulimia is akin to compulsive shopping because it involves binging on food, just as the addicted spender goes on shopping binges. Afterward, the guilt can be so great as to lead to depression and anxiety, causing the bulimic to purge. If you are predisposed to bulimia or overeating, you should be extra watchful of your pace in winding down your compulsive shopping, so that withdrawal does not lead you into an eating disorder.

Kim made a point of staying in touch with Marie and encouraged her to return to the group, which she eventually did. I suggested to Marie that she go into private therapy to deal with the history behind her addictive personality. The severity of her bulimia motivated her to take this advice, and she now sees a psychologist twice a week in addition to coming to the group.

Marie's story raises the important issue of cross-addiction. If you have an addictive personality, and you haven't thoroughly dealt with the reasons why you need this type of escape, you may be vulnerable to serial or multiple addictions. You may give up compulsive shopping only to find yourself drinking or eating too much. You might also manifest several addictive behaviors at one time. Some compulsive shoppers also have eating disorders, drinking or drug addictions, or gambling compulsions.

You need to ask yourself honestly: Do I have any other addictions besides shopping? As I curb my shopping habits, do I see hints of another addiction emerging? If the answer is yes to either of these questions, you should seek out private therapy to supplement the self-help program in this book.

Kim

The group provided a much-needed sense of family for Kim. She had spent so much time among jet-setters, it was important for her to get to know people who led more grounded lives. She also learned that friendships didn't have to be based on wild nights in discos or expensive restaurants. It was the quality of the relationships, not the surroundings, that mattered.

Kim worked near Richard, so they started having lunches together in order to stay away from the stores. They developed a deep platonic friendship that was a learning experience for both. "It was important for me to realize that a guy could like me just for me, not just because I was sexy. I see Richard when I'm wearing my old sweatclothes and no makeup, and he likes me just as much as when I'm dolled up," said Kim.

When Kim came to the group, she still had a great urge to spend and felt very deprived that she no longer had a fortune. Richard helped her cultivate alternate forms of gratification. They would do things together that didn't involve much spending, such as cooking a spaghetti dinner and having friends over or bike-riding in the country. She learned that fun didn't have to be expensive, and a good conversation with friends could be more stimulating and fulfilling than a night on the town. For the first time in both Richard's and Kim's lives, they had companionship based on mutual respect and caring.

Healing often comes from something as basic as having close friends. Good friendships are a core need that is not being met in many compulsive shoppers' lives, causing them to feel even more alienated. By cultivating friendships, they begin to learn what intimacy is all about. This inevitably leads to deeper intimacy in romantic relationships.

Perhaps because they shared the weekly group experience, Kim and Richard found they could be more honest with each other than they had been with others. This honesty meant talking about their innermost fears, as well as their dreams. "I never thought a guy would really like me if I let it all hang out," said Kim. "But Richard taught me that a guy could. Now I have a new boyfriend and I'm being totally honest with him. And you know what? He respects me and likes me more for it. I think this really might be the one."

Kim found that friendship filled up her life in a much more satisfying way than shopping. "I hardly shop at all now. I already have enough to last me a long time. Sometimes someone will say, 'Where'd you get that gorgeous outfit?' when I'm wearing a dress from Paris. When I tell them, it sounds so glamorous, but the truth is there was so much pain behind that crazy lifestyle. I'm much happier now."

Richard

Richard was defensive when he first joined the group, but its support gave him the security he needed to admit that he had a serious spending problem. The group served as a surrogate family with whom he could share his feelings as he never had before. He learned to open up, to admit his vulnerabilities and disappointments and to accept them.

"In the advertising biz it seems like everyone's out to impress, and people just don't talk about their weaknesses or worries," he said. "When I first joined the group, it blew my mind that people were willing to admit things were wrong. But when I finally started talking honestly too, it felt great, like all that bottled-up steam could escape."

Richard was very thorough about doing his "homework." He diligently made his lists and organized his possessions. He reviewed his finances and set up repayment schedules with his creditors. He practiced relaxation, visualization and affirmations at home. "At first a cynical voice in my head kept saying, 'It won't work.' But I kept trying and I started to believe in myself," he said.

Richard had run himself into such a deep financial hole that he had little cash or credit to spend at the onset of his recovery program. Except for necessities, he had to stop shopping completely. He even sold his extra cameras. After five weeks of shopping abstinence, however, he had a setback. He cashed a paycheck and went on a spending spree.

"When I got home I felt really miserable," he said. But instead of just wallowing in it, I started writing about it in my journal. The words kept flowing out, and I filled up pages and pages. I wrote about my mother and my father and things I hadn't thought about in years. Then I called up Kim and asked her to come over. We read the journal together, and we both started crying. I hadn't cried so much since my mother died. We talked for hours. I never thought I could open up so much with a woman. It made me realize I don't have to always keep up a strong facade. If I can let go like this with a friend, maybe I can do the same with a girlfriend. I'm certainly willing to give it a try.

"We cried a lot, but it was a happy kind of sadness. I felt better afterward, better than I had in a long time. Something clicked that day and I let go of a lot. And I haven't overspent since then. That was four months ago."

Anne

Support from the group gave Anne the security she needed to face her family issues. She learned how to communicate with them in a more loving and less angry manner. Of course, they were much more responsive to her new ways of dealing with them than they had been to her bitter outbursts. Josh began to respond to her concern and improve his attitude, and Jeff agreed to marital therapy.

"The group made me aware that I shouldn't have the attitude that I was right and Jeff was wrong, and therapy would prove that. I should be willing to compromise and listen. I guess Jeff picked up on my attitude, because after a while he dropped his defenses and started to communicate in a way he never had before," said Anne.

Once Anne felt that her husband was truly listening to her, much of her bitterness and need for revenge through overspending diminished. So did her snopping. After five months of marital therapy and seven months in the group, her binges were a thing of the past. She decided she would continue coming to the group once a month for several months. "I need the positive reinforcement. Listening to others makes me realize how far I've come," she explained.

Members of the group incorporate whatever techniques they find helpful as a permanent feature of their lives. Anne finds the relaxation exercises indispensable. She taught them to her husband. "Jeff was surprised at how much he enjoyed doing the progressive relaxation," said Anne. "It opened him up to trying new things. We took a couples' massage course at the 'Y' and now we give each other massages. We're not only working on our marriage, we're playing more, too. I still tend to get hyped up, so I figure the more ways I can relax, the less likely I am to binge."

Lisa

By the time Lisa joined the group, she had already consolidated her debts and been forced to admit the extent of her shopping addiction. She entered with a lot of commitment and flung herself enthusiastically into all the self-help activities. She stopped shopping compulsively in only three weeks, an atypically short time.

Then she went through a withdrawal period, during which she became depressed. "Partly it was not shopping anymore, partly it was dredging up a lot of unhappy memories. Anyway, I was really depressed. My checklist read 'low, low, low' every day for a couple of weeks," she said.

Lisa didn't resort to shopping to lift her spirits, however. She turned to the other group members for help. "I would call one of them almost every day. I was afraid of being a bother, but they kept assuring me it was okay. Having them to talk to really saved me," she said.

The group encouraged Lisa to see a psychotherapist to work out the trauma of being molested as a child. After a few weeks of counseling, she started to live more in the present and less in the past. She became closer to Kevin and their marriage improved.

Lisa and Kevin started spending more "play time" together. They took up tennis, took long walks in the country, and started a couples club that met socially once a month. "In a way it was like falling in love all over again—only better. This time I felt like I really deserved his love," she said.

Lisa left the group after seven months, but she kept in touch periodically. She reported only two small shopping sprees over the next six months. She was paying off her consolidated loan faster than she had expected because of her self-discipline. She and Kevin are doing well and they are thinking of having a baby. •

*Since I have my shopping under control, I find so many other ways to fill my time. My volunteer work has given my life the sense of purpose that shopping never could.—**Olivia***

Chapter 10

Spending Less, Living More

When you read the last chapter, you may have been thinking, "They could do it, but can I?" The answer is yes! The group members didn't all start with extraordinary discipline, courage or faith. They had the same doubts you might be experiencing. Yet each of their stories illustrates the strength and perseverance of the human spirit. They were able to overcome addiction with commitment and support.

Support is one of the essential elements of recovery. Think carefully about who will be your "buddy" and provide you with the support you need. Perhaps there is a close friend in whom you can confide. If you are shy about doing this, remember that honesty deepens friendship, and friendship itself is healing. Your spouse or other loved ones can also provide valuable support. In some instances, a sibling or parent might be a good person to turn to. It is ideal if you can set up a small network of supportive people in your life. Also, if you were attracted by the description of the group's activities, you might want to start your own support group.

Starting a Support Group

Before you start a support group in your area, you may want to determine if one already exists. Many communities have an organization that serves as a clearinghouse for self-help groups and carries a list of all self-help groups in the area. The United Way serves as a self-help clearinghouse in some regions. Another good resource to check is your local National Association of Social Workers. One of the best and most frequently ignored resources is your local library. It has many references regarding local community activities, including support groups. Often community churches and synagogues can offer direction. Community bulletin boards are another place to check.

If you find that no support group for compulsive shoppers exists in your area, you may want to start your own. Starting your own group takes time and work, but it can be well worth the effort. Not only will you receive benefits from the group, your self-respect will be enhanced by your efforts to organize it. It will also keep you busy and out of the stores.

A support group can start small—even with you and only one other person. You might mention your shopping compulsion to some friends and see if they say, "Oh, I do that, too," or "I know someone with that problem." Then you can say to the appropriate person something such as, "I was thinking about getting together with some other people to talk about our spending problems and work on them. Would you like to join us, or do you know anyone who would?" Keep the approach light, without mentioning the word "addiction" at first. If someone turns down your invitation, remember that it is not a personal rejection. It probably means that the person is still in the denial mode.

If you wish to expand your group beyond the word-of-mouth range, there are several ways to do this. You can list your group with a self-help clearinghouse. You might consider preparing a flier saying something along the lines of: "Support Group for Compulsive Shoppers Forming," or "Do you have a problem with spending too much money? Call about our new support group." Include either a phone number or a mailing address where you can be contacted. However, in order to maintain privacy, do not include your full name. If you want to maintain complete anonymity, you can take out a post office box number instead of using your home address. Copy the flier and put it up on community bulletin boards. Another way to get members is to take out a small, similarly worded advertisement in a local newspaper.

When people contact you, it might be best to arrange the first meeting in a public place. Because some people you meet will not be appropriate for the group, it is best to say at the onset, "It has been suggested to me that I not give my full name, address or telephone number until I have established a group."

During initial meetings with prospective group members, take down basic information such as name, address and telephone number. You will want to determine whether a shopping compulsion is their major problem, or whether they also have other serious emotional issues to deal with such as divorce, cross-addictions or depression. Try to gauge whether or not people you meet are exceptionally hostile or seriously emotionally disturbed.

After each interview, use the following criteria to determine whether or not the individual belongs in your group:

- If the person admits that a shopping addiction is only one of his or her major problems, the individual should agree to be in individual psychotherapy as a prerequisite to joining the group. Explain that psychotherapy will give the person a chance to deal with other issues so he or she can concentrate on recovery from shopping addiction and provide support for others in the group.
- If the individual seems unduly hostile, do not call him or her back. There is no place for extreme hostility in a self-help support group. Any form of extreme aggression—verbal or physical—is taboo. This needs to be stated also to those who become members of your group.
- If a prospective group member appears to be seriously emotionally disturbed, your group is not appropriate for that individual. These people need a degree of care and attention that only professionals can provide. Because as a lay person you cannot appropriately suggest that they need professional care, it is advisable that you not call them back. This same rule applies to very hostile people. This may seem callous, but there are no other reasonable options.

Some problems that people experience are outside the scope of your group. While your support group is not for everyone, it is difficult for you to be in the position of making judgments about the suitability of people who want to join. However, it is obviously necessary to do so in order to organize a group that will meet the needs of its members.

A group of six to ten people is optimal, but flexibility is important. Once you have a group of people ready to commit to recovery, call them back and arrange a time and place for the first meeting. The meetings should take place once a week for at least an hour and a half. It is better to hold your meetings in a public place than in individual homes. This lends a more task-oriented mood to the meetings without eliminating the social dimensions that are crucial to the recovery process.

If there's a branch of the United Way in your area, it can be helpful in locating free or reasonably priced space for meetings. Churches and synagogues are often happy to supply space or direct you to available rooms elsewhere. Local schools, Y's, community centers and libraries are other good possibilities for a meeting place. You can probably find space for free, but if not, ask group members to contribute equally to the cost of the space.

Many formal groups have charters. Although a charter is not necessary for your group, you might want to present rules either verbally or in writing. The basic rules are:

- Members should come to the meetings on time.
- Members should come to each weekly meeting unless circumstances truly prevent them from attending.
- Members should be supportive of one another and available for participation in the buddy system.
- Ideally, members should commit to attending the meetings for the eight weeks of the recovery program, and at least two months afterward.

You might find it helpful to have a mental-health professional join your group each week, biweekly or once a month. Most communities have a mental-health organization that can put you in contact with psychiatrists, psychologists, social workers, counselors and other practitioners. Having a professional present can make the members feel more secure, increase their faith in the group and speed recovery. The group can decide with the mental-health worker what role he or she will play. The professional can be an active leader or simply sit in and listen, making only occasional suggestions or interpretations.

Although having a mental-health worker participate in your group is desirable, it is not necessary. If you live in a part of the country where such a person is not available, or you and the other members cannot afford to pay the professional, do not let this deter you from starting a group. A support group of peers who share a common problem can be quite helpful.

You can run your group any way you wish, of course. However, the program outlined in this book has been proven effective, and following its guidelines will make your group successful.

The Post-Recovery Program

After all the hard work of recovery, you will want to be careful not to lapse back into addiction. You can help prevent this by permanently incorporating some of the recovery techniques into your lifestyle.

Chaos in any area of your life can lead to confusion, anxiety and compulsion, so you should continue to keep your possessions in order. Maintain your lists for at least two years after recovery, and keep them with you when you shop. If you find this is a valuable tool, you may want to employ it indefinitely. These decisions are up to you. More often than not, it will become habitual if you maintain organization. Try to keep your financial affairs in order as well. If you need to, hire a bookkeeper or accountant one day a month to help you. It's worth the effort for the peace of mind.

All your credit cards should be permanently eliminated except one, a type which has to be paid back every month. Even that one should always be left at home when you shop. If you are shopping for a costly item, you should go over your budget first, then bring one check to the store. Otherwise, use cash. Remember, in order to remain a recovered compulsive shopper, you have to withstand the seduction of credit-card shopping.

Some of the recovery techniques can become as much a part of your daily routine as brushing your teeth. Because stress is inevitable, continuing to practice progressive relaxation once a day—or at least several times a week—is helpful. Keep in touch with your body, and it will tell you when it needs the practice most. Besides reducing the tension that can lead to compulsion, relaxation techniques will benefit your physical health over the years. They can make you look and feel younger. Also, the breathing relaxation technique is so simple and portable that you can always employ it during stressful situations.

Creative visualizations have even greater potential than helping you overcome compulsive shopping. They can help you achieve many diverse goals. Affirmations can be used hand-in-hand with visualizations to begin positive changes in a multitude of ways, such as improving your love life, healing physical ailments or increasing self-confidence. The more you use these methods, the more you'll experience their profound power.

You may not want to keep a daily checklist or write in your journal forever. However, you may, because you enjoy the self-discovery and renewal that is brings. If you stop writing, try to remain aware of what you're thinking, feeling and experiencing. It is easy to get so caught up in the daily grind that you lose touch with your inner self.

You will want to continue cultivating new relationships and activities that enrich your life. The fuller your life is, the less you need to fill it with purchases. The busier you are with enjoyable and satisfying pursuits, the less time you have to spend in the stores. However, you don't want to "overload your circuits" and become so busy that it causes you anxiety. Quiet, relaxing moments are necessary to refuel yourself. We all have to find our own comfort zone and strike a balance between doing and being. You'll be able to do this best if you keep checking in with yourself, noticing how you feel both physically and mentally, as the two are inextricably linked.

When you are not feeling happy and well, remember: you don't have to shop your way out of the blues. At this point, you are too self-aware and resourceful. Instead, take stock of your life to discover what is making you dissatisfied. This may be painful, but you've done this before and are strong enough to bear the discomfort. Be kind, gentle and accepting with yourself, and you can grow and learn from self-examination.

Take positive actions, backed by affirmations and visualizations, to change whatever situation is dragging you down. For example, if you are not getting what you want from a relationship, talk to the person involved. The more honestly you communicate, the richer and more satisfying your life will be. Devote your energy to achieving a sense of accomplishment, not to pointless spending. Your worth does not come from what you buy, it comes from the meaningful, joyous life you are capable of creating for yourself. •

Footnotes

• • • • • • • • • •

Introduction

[1]Morris, Betsey, "Big Spenders," *The Wall Street Journal,* Vol. CCX, No. 22, July 30, 1987, pp. 1, 13.

[2]Morris, Betsey, "Big Spenders," *The Wall Street Journal,* Vol. CCX, No. 22, pp. 1, 13.

[3]Leary, Brian, "Should We Have Credit Cards?," *Parade Magazine,* April 5, 1987, pp. 28-29.

[4]Asnes, Marion, "Managing Your Money," *Vogue,* Vol. 177, No. 9, September 1987, p. 271.

[5]Leary, Brian, "Should We Have Credit Cards?," *Parade Magazine,* April 5, 1987, pp. 28-29.

Chapter Six

[1]Tavris, Carol. *Anger: The Misunderstood Emotion.* New York: Simon & Schuster, 1984, p. 49.